# Sticky, Chewy, Messy, Gooey

## DESSERTS FOR THE SERIOUS SWEET TOOTH

• • •

By Jill O'Connor

PHOTOGRAPHS BY LEIGH BEISCH

CHRONICLE BOOKS

SAN FRANCISCO

## DEDICATION

• • •

For my favorite sugar babies, Olivia and Sophia, and for Jim, who makes my life so sweet.

## ACKNOWLEDGMENTS

• • •

It would be impossible to finish a project as absorbing and time-consuming as writing a book without the understanding, enthusiasm, and willing tastebuds of my husband and two very sweet daughters. Thanks, too, to Sandi Burke, Heather Tynch, and Cambi Martin for their invaluable assistance and good humor. Thanks to Denise Gee for helping me unravel the mysteries of whiskey and to Nancie McDermott for her advice on cracking coconuts, her memory of the Poky Little Puppy, and her hilarious e-mails when the going got tough. Thanks to my parents for giving me free rein in the kitchen growing up, and to Vicki Villarreal and Nancy Bowen, who were the first to actually hire me and pay me to cook. Finally, many thanks to Bill LeBlond and Amy Treadwell, for their support and encouragement in making this sticky, chewy book a reality; to Carrie Bradley for her gentle editing, and to Ayako Akazawa, Leigh Beisch, Dan Becker, and Sara Slavin for making everything look so beautiful.

Text copyright © 2007 by JILL O'CONNOR.
Photographs copyright © 2007 by LEIGH BEISCH.
All rights reserved. No part of this book may be reproduced in any form without written permission from the publisher.

Library of Congress Cataloging-in-Publication Data available.

ISBN-10: 0-8118-5566-X
ISBN-13: 978-0-8118-5566-2

Manufactured in China.

Designed by AYAKO AKAZAWA
Food styling by DAN BECKER
Prop styling by SARA SLAVIN
Typesetting by JANIS REED

The photographer wishes to thank the entire photo team that worked with her on this project, especially Sara Slavin for her amazing sense of style and fantastic array of props and Dan Becker for his hard work and creativity. She also wishes to thank Ayako Akazawa for her constant enthusiasm and support.

10 9 8 7 6 5 4 3

Chronicle Books LLC
680 Second Street
San Francisco, California 94107
www.chroniclebooks.com

# Introduction

 *"I can resist everything except temptation."*
—OSCAR WILDE

Who wouldn't want to enter the fantastical world of Willy Wonka and his wonderful chocolate factory full of violet-flavored marshmallows and "little feathery sweets that melt away deliciously the moment you put them between your lips"? There, food isn't just sustenance. It is adventure. It is magic. It is abundance, luxury, and excess, all tied up into one big, pink, innocent bow of childlike glee. That is the world I want to re-create with the recipes in this book. Just like the aromas wafting from Wonka's chocolate factory, sweets oozing with sticky chewy caramel and butterscotch, gooey with marshmallows and jam, dripping with cream and dribbled with chocolate entice us to indulge our inner Augustus Gloop—if only every now and then. I loved reading about food when I was growing up. I was drawn to the kitchen, to the pleasure and romance of cooking and eating, as much from reading books as I was from the food actually cooking in my own childhood kitchen. All my favorite stories kept me in thrall through the descriptions of the real and imaginary foods eaten and prepared. I always smiled imagining Winnie-the-Pooh's great golden paw dipping into his pots of honey, or the Poky Little Puppy lapping up rice pudding when he finally makes it home to his mother. At the end of *Bread and Jam for Frances*, Frances digs in to the school lunch to end all school lunches, complete with lobster salad sandwiches (on thin slices of white bread) and, among other things, "two plums and a tiny basket of cherries. And vanilla pudding with chocolate sprinkles and a spoon to eat it with." Whew. No wonder she and her friend Albert decide "eating is nice." I remember finding an article in one

of my mother's cooking magazines with a detailed menu and recipes for a Christmas breakfast just like the one the March sisters gave up to the poor German family in *Little Women*, complete with sizzling, crisp-skinned sausages wrapped in buckwheat pancakes. I wanted to make it on the spot—with real maple syrup, not the pancake syrup in the log-cabin-shaped bottle we stored in the refrigerator door. I wanted to fry my own donuts after reading about the heady, all-but-bacchanalian feasts Almanzo Wilder tucked in to throughout the whole of *Farmer Boy,* which I know had a plot, but all I can remember was how much food that boy could put away. The description of donuts frying is sheer heaven: "they . . . went to the bottom, sending up bubbles. Then quickly they came popping up, to float and slowly swell till they rolled themselves over, their pale golden backs going into the fat and their plump brown bellies rising out of it." That book is one big feast of custard, pumpkin, and spicy apple pie "with its thick, rich juice and its crumbly crust"; preserves and jams and jellies; rivers of real maple syrup; and those donuts, hot and crisp from the fryer. I was transfixed by the description of Laura Ingalls's first taste of horehound candy. It sounded exotic and fabulous and completely unattainable, and I obsessed about tasting it for a long time, until I happened one day to visit an old-fashioned candy store selling a big selection of swirled ribbon candy, toast-colored chunks of maple sugar pressed into the shape of maple leaves, and jar upon jar of colored candy sticks in every flavor and color imaginable. Then I saw them. Unassuming little sugar-dusted, taupe lozenges in a small bag marked "horehound drops." I couldn't believe it! I was sure they would transport me to another place and time. I was so excited. I passed by my favorite red licorice and the crunchy little sugar drops they sell on long sheets of paper, like tiny pills on a page, and with great excitement I purchased a bag then and there. I still remember the bitter disappointment, and the malty, cough-syrup flavor of those horehound drops. Some real-life experiences can never live up to their imaginary predecessors. Reading *The Secret Garden* started my long love affair with England, and I wanted to have a picnic with Dickon, Mary, and Colin and dine on "roasted eggs and potatoes and richly frothed milk and oat-cakes and buns and heather honey and clotted cream." It was years before I actually tasted real clotted cream in Devon, England; pale and creamy and thick as mayonnaise but mildly sweet, piled four inches high in a thick pottery bowl to spread on scones with homemade strawberry jam. Unlike the horehound drops in my story, clotted cream is sure to exceed any fantasy you may have about it. Traveling in my mind from the English countryside to the fairy-tale forests of old Europe to the American prairie and farm country and back again, I licked imaginary cones of frozen custard while visiting the fair with Wilbur and Templeton and Charlotte from *Charlotte's Web*, fried hundreds of donuts with Almanzo's mother, nibbled on the gingerbread house with "marchpane windows" along with Hansel and Gretel, and tucked into Jam Roly-Poly and berries and thick cream with Beatrix Potter. My mother used to complain that she had to take my books away from me while I was growing up so we could have a real conversation. So when just reading about all this fabulous food was no longer enough, I pulled my nose from my books and followed it to the kitchen to cook up some magic of my own. I began, of course, with dessert, because baking has a magic all its own. Nothing delights the eye and encourages you to live only in the moment like a rich, frothy sweet: a gooey brownie layered with walnuts and strands of chewy caramel, a crisp wedge of buttery shortbread, an ice cream sundae slathered with homemade butterscotch and caramel sauces, a cupcake. One of the first cookbooks I was given was called *The Pooh Cook Book*. I tried to make Honey

Toffee Pennies and scorched the caramel so badly it filled the kitchen with the bitter, acrid smell of burnt sugar for days. I learned quickly what color amber is—and it isn't black. After the toffee pennies, I got better. I went on to successfully bake chewy seven-layer bars, Swedish cinnamon sand cookies, pans of brownies, elaborate bûches de Noël, and German chocolate cakes. I collected recipes from the mothers of my friends and, of course, read book after book after book. I discovered there is no satisfaction sweeter than the "oohs" and "aahs" elicited by a beautifully presented, delicious dessert. Eyes light up and everybody smiles when you walk into the dining room carrying something glistening with chocolate or covered in cream. Is it any wonder, then, that I always think, in life, there is no trouble a little butter and a lot of chocolate can't make better? If you have a real sweet tooth, you probably feel the same way. Since you have obviously cracked the spine of a book entitled *Sticky, Chewy, Messy, Gooey*, I am going to assume you are the devil-may-care type. One who can fearlessly enter my world of chocolate, butterscotch, and marshmallows with a gutsy, guilt-free, take-no-prisoners sense of abandon, ready to trek through these sugar-speckled, cream-drenched pages to find your favorite. If you share my philosophy of "if some is good, more is better," than this is definitely the book for you. But there are memories here, as well. Recipes inspired by stories, traveling, and dreams, where calories don't matter and all that is important is the pleasure of the moment; moments discovering new tastes and textures and flavors; and the resonating joy of sharing something delicious with someone you love. Let's make some magic.

"All the most wonderful smells in the world seemed to be mixed up in the air around them—the smell of roasting coffee and burnt sugar and melting chocolate and mint and violets and crushed hazelnuts and apple blossoms and caramel and lemon peel."
—FROM *CHARLIE AND THE CHOCOLATE FACTORY*, BY ROALD DAHL.

# Ingredients

I try to make sure most of the ingredients I use in my recipes can be found in well-stocked grocery stores. Check the Internet for a few items that may be slightly harder to find.

**BUTTER:** There is no substitute for butter. I like the fresh taste of unsalted butter best. It is also easier to control the salt content in a recipe if the butter is unsalted. There is no need to purchase fancy imported or extra-fat butters—ordinary unsalted butter is just fine.

**CHOCOLATE:** Most of my recipes using chocolate call for semisweet or bittersweet. I often use Lindt, along with Hershey's Dark, Scharffen Berger, and Guittard brands. As these quality chocolates become more popular, they are more and more available in many grocery stores. Other popular European brands such as Callebaut and Valrhona are available in some larger grocery stores, in specialty-food stores like Williams-Sonoma, or from mail-order sources or online. I tried all these chocolates when testing the recipes here, and they were all successful. One thing to remember when choosing your chocolate is to check the chocolate percentage, if it is listed. The higher the percentage of chocolate, the lower the sugar content. I found for most of my recipes, semisweet chocolates around 60 percent were the most successful in taste as well as temperament. If you want to try the higher-percentage chocolates, do not go over 70 to 72 percent, as the chocolate may become more unstable when heated and be too bitter for most tastes. When using chocolate chips, I always reach for the bright yellow bag of Nestlé Toll House semisweet chocolate morsels. If you choose a different brand, just make sure the label reads "real semisweet chocolate." See page 20 for more information on chocolate.

**COCOA POWDER:** Both "natural" and "Dutch-processed" cocoa powders are used in the recipes here. The most popular brand of natural cocoa powder is Hershey's Cocoa. Natural cocoa is very acidic and is a popular choice for traditional American recipes, usually leavened with baking soda, which may also include other acidic ingredients like buttermilk and sour cream to highlight natural cocoa's deep chocolate flavor. Dutch-processed cocoa, also called alkalized cocoa, is called for in many European recipes. It is darker, richer, and milder than its American counterpart, and is often used in recipes with less sugar or without chemical leavening agents. It is also the best cocoa powder to use for sprinkling over cakes, truffles, or other desserts as a garnish. Callebaut, Valrhona, and Bensdorp all make excellent Dutch-processed cocoa powder.

**COCONUT:** I use many different kinds of coconut in my recipes, including sweetened shredded coconut, unsweetened flaked coconut, and desiccated (or macaroon) coconut. All are available in grocery stores and natural-food markets, and they all have very different flavors and textures. Fresh coconuts are usually available year-round, but are at their best from October to December. See page 78 for more information on coconut.

**DAIRY PRODUCTS:** I used whole milk exclusively for the recipes in this book. You can substitute low-fat (but not nonfat, please!) milk if you like, but there may be a difference in the richness and texture of the final dessert. Low-fat or nonfat buttermilk is fine to use, but when using sour cream and cream cheese, choose only the full-fat variety. I use heavy cream, not whipping cream, when cream is called for. It has a slightly higher fat content and therefore a richer flavor. Heavy cream also seems to whip faster and stay firmer without deflating. For the freshest flavor, try to find cream without any additives such as carrageenan or pectin, which are added to make the cream seem thicker. Check the ingredients list on the back of the container and choose a brand with the fewest additives.

**EGGS:** Use large eggs for the best results with these recipes. Large eggs weigh about 2 ounces each, so you can weigh your eggs, if you like, to ensure accuracy.

**EXTRACTS:** Always use extracts labeled "pure." Never use imitation vanilla, almond, or peppermint extracts especially, as their flavor will be either bland or have a harsh chemical aftertaste.

**FLOUR:** For accuracy, I tested most of the recipes in this book using national brands Pillsbury and Gold Medal flour. I call variously for bleached or unbleached all-purpose flour or cake flour, depending on the desired properties for each finished baked good. See page 114 for more information on types of flour.

**MARSHMALLOW FLUFF:** This trademark sweet, creamy concoction is the epitome of gooey desserts. I like to add it to sandwiches, meringues, candies, and cake icings. It is worth adding to your grocery list, or, if you are like me and live in California or other points west of the Rockies, mail-order a case to keep in your earthquake survival kit!

**NUTS:** For the freshest flavor, I prefer to buy whole shelled nuts (or shelled halves for walnuts and pecans) that I toast and chop myself. Almonds and hazelnuts can be purchased raw (with their skins) or blanched (skinned). Store nuts in the freezer, double bagged, to extend their shelf life and prevent them from going rancid. Nuts should be chopped first and then toasted, just before they are needed, for maximum flavor. See page 89 for more information on nuts.

**SPIRITS:** Bake with the same high-quality spirits you would be happy to drink. Some of my favorites are Grand Marnier, bourbon whiskey, and Irish whiskey. Dark rum, Kahlúa, Armagnac and Cognac, kirsch, calvados and poire Williams, Chambord, and amaretto are also delicious. Flavored vodkas, from orange and raspberry to chocolate and vanilla, can also be added to your repertoire. To limit the expense, buy larger bottles of your favorites that you enjoy drinking and cooking with often; for more unusual choices, stock up on tiny bottles. If you enjoy the flavor in the recipe, you can then consider investing in a larger bottle to add to your bar.

**SUGAR:** Stick with pure cane, granulated, superfine, light and dark brown, and powdered, or confectioners', sugars. Dark and light muscovado sugars and raw demerara and turbinado sugars are also delicious choices. See page 73 for more information on types of sugar.

# Equipment

The following equipment will help make the stickiest, gooiest desserts a possibility in your kitchen. I start with The Basics: equipment and tools every baker needs in their kitchen. The Beyond Basics section includes specialty equipment, tools, or baking pans that may not be used every day but are essential to the success of certain dishes.

## The Basics

### PANS AND BOWLS

**BAKING PANS, SQUARE AND RECTANGULAR:** Most of the bar cookies in this book are made in a straight-sided, aluminum 9-by-13-inch pan. Eight- or 9-inch square baking dishes are also useful for smaller-batch baking. These are versatile, inexpensive, and indestructible. You may also want to invest in at least one oval or rectangular ceramic 9-by-13-inch pan for bread puddings or other desserts you can serve straight from the pan.

**BAKING SHEETS:** Start with at least two heavy aluminum rimmed baking sheets, often called half-sheets. Available in restaurant supply and kitchenware stores, they are versatile and inexpensive. I also like to have at least one rimless, insulated baking sheet. These sheets diffuse the heat of the oven and protect delicate cookies or pastries and keep them from burning or browning excessively. Having both rimmed and rimless baking sheets is important—sometime a rim is required to keep gooey foods from dripping onto the oven floor as they bake while rimless pans make it easy to slide cookies and the like onto cooling racks.

**CAKE PANS:** Round, straight-sided aluminum cake pans are inexpensive and heavy-duty. Pans that are 2 to 3 inches deep are the best choice. They are available in kitchenware shops, restaurant supply stores, and anywhere cake-decorating supplies are sold. Start with 8-inch, 9-inch, and/or 10-inch sizes, purchasing two of any size for making layer cakes.

**LOAF PANS:** Start with two nonstick 8½-by-4½-inch pans. Larger 9-by-5-inch pans are also handy.

**MIXING BOWLS:** You should have at least one large and one small glass or ceramic bowl for use in the microwave for melting butter or chocolate, but I can't get enough stainless-steel mixing bowls. They are inexpensive and very useful. They come in a variety of sizes, often in nested sets, and are very durable and lightweight, as well as heat-resistant. They can be heated, chilled, and frozen with no complaints and won't chip like ceramic bowls or melt in the dishwasher like plastic bowls can. They are available in restaurant-supply stores; fancy kitchenware shops; discount stores like Kmart, Wal-Mart, and Target; and even some grocery stores. True workhorses, these bowls will never let you down.

**MUFFIN PANS:** Two 12-cup, nonstick standard-size muffin pans should enable you to make cupcakes and muffins to your heart's content. Two nonstick mini-muffin pans give the option of bite-size muffins, and can sometimes substitute for financier or madeleine pans (see page 13).

**PIE PANS:** Glass pie pans, such as Pyrex, are inexpensive and durable. Glass is a great conductor of heat and delivers crisp, evenly-browned crusts. It is also easier to see how brown the crust is getting with a glass pan. One or two 9-inch pans are good to start with.

**SAUCEPANS:** Invest in a small set of straight-sided, heavy-bottomed stainless-steel saucepans in these sizes: 1-quart, 2-quart, and 3-quart, with matching lids. Also useful is a Dutch oven or a large, deep skillet for pan-frying and deep-frying.

**TUBE AND BUNDT PANS:** The classic shape of these pans features a central tube that helps the center of certain kinds of cakes to rise and bake evenly. Angel food cake pans, with a simple, smooth-sided design, sometimes have removable bottoms and small "feet" that allow the inverted pan to stand clear of the center during cooling. Bundt pans are typically fluted, with fixed bottoms and no feet, and are excellent for pretty pound cakes, rum cakes, and other plain or glazed cakes. I have a whole collection of different designs for every season and occasion. I recommend starting with one Bundt pan and one regular tube pan.

## TOOLS AND UTENSILS

**ELECTRIC MIXER:** An inexpensive kitchen basic, electric mixers take the elbow grease out of making cake batters, whipped cream, and egg foams. A small, sturdy hand mixer may often be more convenient than a large free-standing mixer for mixing and beating together smaller quantities of ingredients.

**FOOD PROCESSOR:** Perfect for chopping nuts, grating coconut, making your own nut flours, puréeing fruit, and preparing various cookie and pastry doughs, the food processor has become a kitchen staple. Inexpensive mini processors are also available and can do many of the chores performed by the more expensive larger models.

**ICING/OFFSET SPATULA:** Thin, flexible metal spatulas with a rounded tip are a must for perfectly icing cakes and cupcakes, and spreading fillings. They come in various lengths—6 inches, 8 inches and 12 inches are the most common. Offset spatulas have an angled blade, making them useful for removing items from a baking sheet or spreading and maneuvering icing into tight places. You should have at least one 6- or 8-inch spatula and one 12-inch spatula.

**KNIVES:** Start with a good-quality 8-inch or 10-inch chef's knife and a paring knife. A serrated knife is also handy for slicing bread and splitting cake layers.

**MEASURING CUPS:** Individual metal or plastic cups in 1-cup, ½-cup, ⅓-cup, and ¼-cup sizes are most accurate for measuring dry ingredients. Use glass or clear plastic 8-ounce or 16-ounce measuring cups for liquids.

**MICROPLANE ZESTER:** These very sharp graters come in a variety of sizes and are perfect for creating piles of fluffy fresh coconut or grating chocolate, fresh nutmeg, or citrus zest. Although you can use a regular box grater for these tasks, the microplane zester is inexpensive and much easier to use.

**OVEN THERMOMETER:** Knowing the exact temperature of your oven will save you a lot of grief. Oven thermometers are inexpensive and an easy guide to any adjustments you need to make if your oven temperature gauge is a little off, to ensure that you are baking at the proper temperature.

**PARCHMENT PAPER AND SILPAT SHEETS:** Parchment paper is a nonstick paper crucial for lining cake pans and baking sheets to keep some mixtures from sticking to the pan. Once hard to find, parchment paper is now readily available where aluminum foil and plastic wrap are sold. Silpat sheets are flat, nonstick, washable, and reusable pads used to line baking sheets. Cake pans, financier molds, Bundt pans, madeleine pans, and other shaped pans are also available made from this material. Nothing sticks to Silpat.

**PASTRY BRUSH:** A natural boar-bristle brush with a wooden handle is best for brushing glazes over tarts, egg washes over pastries, or melted butter over dough. Buy two brushes: one for butter and oil, and one for egg washes, fruit glazes, or brushing water down the sides of a pot of boiling caramel.

**ROLLING PIN:** There are many types of rolling pins available, but my two favorites are the large French pins without handles (similar to large wooden dowels) and the old-fashioned spinning pin with wooden handles. Both work well, so choose the one that you find most comfortable to handle. I find marble pins too heavy, but you may want to test-drive one; many bakers opt for these.

**RUBBER AND HEATPROOF SILICONE SPATULAS:** Heatproof silicone is an improvement over old-fashioned rubber spatulas. Silicone remains stain-free and won't absorb food odors. Flat and/or spoon-shaped spatulas are necessities for folding ingredients together and scraping the last bit of batter from the bowl. Invest in at least one flat and one spoon-shaped spatula to best cover all baking needs.

**SIEVES:** Available in different capacities and sizes of weave, mesh sieves are used for tasks like straining custards and sifting flour, cocoa, and confectioners' sugar. Coarse-meshed wire sieves are most useful for quickly sifting dry ingredients. Fine-meshed or plastic sieves are great for straining custards and sauces because they won't cause the custard to discolor or give it a metallic aftertaste.

**WIRE RACK:** One or two flat wire cooling racks are necessary for cooling cookies, cakes, and other baked goods.

**WIRE WHISKS:** Whisks are available in many sizes and shapes. Start with one large, round balloon whisk for whipping air into foods including egg whites, sauces, and cream. You should also have at least one longer, narrower whisk with stiffer wires, sometimes called a piano whisk—these are useful for beating heavier ingredients together and preventing lumps from forming in cooked custards or sauces.

**WOODEN SPOONS:** These kitchen-classic spoons are inexpensive and versatile, and when stirring hot caramel sauces, they are essential. I like to have as many as possible, but you should have at least three or four, so you can stir more than one sauce at a time, I also find them the perfect tool for propping open the oven door to release excess heat. Nothing feels as good as a wooden spoon in your hand. Furthermore, they won't scrape or damage your pots and pans, and the handle stays cool when you're stirring hot custards and sauces.

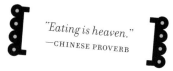

*"Eating is heaven."*
—CHINESE PROVERB

## Beyond Basics

### PANS AND MOLDS

**MADELEINE PAN:** The standard madeleine pan has 12 or 20 small, shell-shaped molds for baking the tender sponge cakes Proust made famous. Similar financier pans have 1-by-2-inch rectangular molds. Either is an extra in your arsenal, but equips you for a venture into the delicious world of classical and fanciful French cookie-cakes.

**PORCELAIN CUSTARD CUPS AND RAMEKINS:** Heavy, heat-resistant custard cups and ramekins are perfect for individual servings of custard, pudding, and pots de crème. Start with at least six 6-ounce cups and work up to a collection of twelve. You can also use heat-proof coffee cups (the smaller ones that come with a saucer, not the larger mugs) for double-duty use as baking vessels. Desserts served in a coffee cup and saucer have a certain charm I am particularly fond of.

**SPRINGFORM PAN:** Straight-sided cake pans with removable sides, springform pans are essential for soft and delicate cakes like cheesecakes, mousse cakes, soufflé cakes, and tortes. Start with a 9-inch round and/or 10-inch round pan.

**TART PAN:** One 9- or 10-inch round tart pan is a good starter pan as an option to a pie pan for creating shallow, elegant pastries. Often they are fluted, for the signature edge. Tart pans with removable sides are optimal for clean unmolding and a pretty presentation.

### TOOLS AND UTENSILS

**BLENDER:** You can't make a milkshake without a good, solid blender. It is also a great tool for puréeing fruit and blending sauces.

**BLOWTORCH:** Mini propane- or butane-powered kitchen torches are used to caramelize the sugar atop crème brûlée or to brown meringue topping when you don't want to use the broiler. These little kitchen-size flamethrowers are especially useful if the dessert you are caramelizing needs to stay cold.

**CANDY THERMOMETER:** Available in many price ranges, from inexpensive grocery-store thermometers to more expensive digital ones from specialty stores, candy thermometers are essential for successful (or at least foolproof) candy making. Personally, I like the digital thermometers—they are easier to read and there is no guesswork involved. See page 154 for more information on temperatures in candy making.

**ICE-CREAM SCOOP:** These come in a variety of sizes and, in addition to the obvious chore of scooping ice cream, they make perfectly proportioned scoops of cookie dough. Choose scoopers equipped with a spring-loaded scraper to take the fuss out of releasing any ingredient.

**PANINI PRESS:** These little gadgets, like a close-and-play countertop grill, are perfect for a variety of crispy, pressed sandwiches both sweet and savory.

**STAND MIXER:** I have a large KitchenAid mixer, and I cannot live without it! This mixer makes meringues, classic butter-creams, and big batches of cookie dough a snap to prepare. With a paddle attachment for cookie and pastry doughs, a whisk attachment to beat creams and egg whites, and a dough hook for kneading bread dough, a basic free-standing mixer pays for itself many times over. Ranging in prices from $200 and up, this piece of equipment is definitely an investment, but if you are a big baker—or want to be—it is worth every penny.

1

Sticky, Chewy
# CHOCOLATE

Have you ever noticed
that there are no "vanillaholics"?
That no one prescribes eating strawberry
ice cream to mend a broken heart, or sends lemon
drops to woo a new lover on Valentine's Day?

Now, I'm not saying that vanilla isn't a wonderful sidekick, even the elusive perfume dabbed behind the ear of every great dessert, or that strawberry ice cream and lemon drops aren't completely delightful—but chocolate is different. Chocolate is special. Chocolate has the power to elicit the passionate devotion of a starry-eyed acolyte. Perhaps it's chocolate's versatility that causes such admiration. Chocolate desserts can be, by turns, elegantly pure—in a dark bittersweet gâteau, thin and unctuously moist, with a sleek layer of ganache glossing its shoulders— or it can be earthy and homey—in a simple walnut-studded fudge brownie, served warm with a big scoop of vanilla ice cream melting dreamily beside it. Whatever incarnation chocolate assumes, from a velvety mousse to a thick-as-pudding cup of hot chocolate to a crisp, buttery cookie to a festive four-layer birthday cake, black with cocoa and topped with loopy swirls of rich buttercream, when it comes to anything chocolate, there really is no substitute. And we just can't get enough.

These brownies are the true definition of sticky, chewy, messy, and gooey. They are so chockablock with gooey extras like chocolate chips, roasted nuts, chunks of melting candy bars, and toasted marshmallows, that I bake them individually in muffin tins to avoid the frustrating chore of trying to cut them into neat little squares.

# Heart of Darkness Brownies

MAKES 24 BROWNIE CUPS

1½ CUPS (3 STICKS) UNSALTED BUTTER

6 OUNCES UNSWEETENED CHOCOLATE

2¼ CUPS GRANULATED SUGAR

1 CUP FIRMLY PACKED LIGHT BROWN SUGAR

6 LARGE EGGS, LIGHTLY BEATEN

1 TABLESPOON PURE VANILLA EXTRACT

1½ CUPS ALL-PURPOSE FLOUR

½ TEASPOON SALT

1 CUP VERY COARSELY CHOPPED RAW ALMONDS OR PECANS, TOASTED (SEE PAGE 89)

1 CUP SEMISWEET CHOCOLATE CHIPS

5 FULL-SIZE (2.07 OUNCES EACH) SNICKERS CANDY BARS, CUT INTO SMALL CHUNKS

3 CUPS MINI MARSHMALLOWS

**FOR THE CARAMEL DRIZZLE:**

6 OUNCES (ABOUT 25) UNWRAPPED CARAMEL CANDIES

2 TABLESPOONS HEAVY CREAM

1 TEASPOON PURE VANILLA EXTRACT

PINCH OF SALT

POSITION A RACK IN THE MIDDLE OF THE OVEN AND PREHEAT TO 350°F. Spray two standard 12-cup muffin tins with nonstick cooking spray.

MELT THE BUTTER AND UNSWEETENED CHOCOLATE TOGETHER IN A SMALL SAUCEPAN OVER MEDIUM-LOW HEAT AND STIR UNTIL SMOOTH. Pour the chocolate mixture into a bowl and stir in the sugars, eggs, and vanilla. Sift the flour and salt into the chocolate mixture and stir just until combined. Stir in the cooled chopped nuts, chocolate chips, and chunks of candy bar.

FILL EACH CUPCAKE CUP HALFWAY WITH BATTER. Bake until the surface of the brownies has a glossy, crackled surface, about 20 minutes. Remove the brownies from the oven and top each one with ¼ cup of the mini marshmallows. Return the brownies to the oven and cook just until the marshmallows start to melt and puff up a bit, but not browned too much, about 2 minutes. Transfer to a wire rack to cool just enough to handle, then remove from the cupcake cups, running a knife around the edge of each brownie to loosen it from the cup. Let cool completely on the wire rack.

WHILE THE BROWNIES ARE COOLING, MAKE THE CARAMEL DRIZZLE: Combine the caramels, cream, vanilla, and salt in a microwave-safe bowl. Microwave, uncovered, on high for 1 minute. Remove from the microwave and stir until smooth. If the caramels are not completely melted, continue heating in 30-second increments, stirring until smooth.

DRIZZLE THE BROWNIES WITH MELTED CARAMEL AND LET COOL COMPLETELY FOR THE CARAMEL TO HARDEN. Do not chill. Serve immediately, or store for up to 3 days in a covered container.

Just the sound of this dessert makes me smile. The thought of slurping up a large spoonful of rich, creamy chocolate—thick and rich as Willy Wonka's magical chocolate waterfall—will make children and adults equally happy. The velvety pound-cake croutons are brushed with melted butter, sprinkled with cinnamon-sugar, and broiled until they are sweet and crispy. I like to use my favorite cream-cheese pound cake recipe, but you can use your own recipe, or purchased pound cake, with equal success. Feel free to use a heart- or star-shaped cookie cutter to give your croutons a fanciful shape.

# Dark Chocolate Soup SERVES 8
# with Cinnamon-Toasted Pound-Cake Croutons

1/2 CUP SUGAR

1/4 CUP WATER

PINCH OF SALT

6 CUPS HALF-AND-HALF

2 TEASPOONS INSTANT ESPRESSO POWDER

1 1/2 POUNDS (24 OUNCES) BITTERSWEET OR SEMISWEET CHOCOLATE, FINELY CHOPPED

8 SMALL SCOOPS VANILLA ICE CREAM

CINNAMON-TOASTED POUND-CAKE CROUTONS (RECIPE FOLLOWS)

COMBINE THE SUGAR AND WATER IN A LARGE SAUCEPAN OVER MEDIUM HEAT. Cook, gently swirling the pan occasionally, until the sugar dissolves and starts to change color. Increase the heat to high and boil until the syrup turns a deep amber color, 4 to 5 minutes. Watch carefully, as it can burn quickly. Immediately remove the pan from the heat and add the salt and half-and-half. Use a long-handled wooden spoon to carefully stir in the half-and-half, as the caramel has a tendency to hiss and splash as the cold cream hits it. Bring the mixture just to a gentle boil, stirring to dissolve the caramel into the half-and-half, about 2 minutes. Remove from the heat and stir in the espresso powder and chopped chocolate. Stir until the chocolate is melted and the mixture is smooth. Divide the soup among 8 shallow soup bowls. Carefully place a scoop of vanilla ice cream in the center of each bowl and float 4 pound-cake croutons around each scoop of ice cream. Serve immediately.

# Cinnamon-Toasted Pound-Cake Croutons MAKES 32 CROUTONS

1 LOAF (8 1/2 BY 4 1/2 INCHES) MY FAVORITE CREAM-CHEESE POUND CAKE (PAGE 37) OR PURCHASED POUND CAKE

1/2 CUP SUGAR

2 TEASPOONS GROUND CINNAMON

1/2 CUP (1 STICK) UNSALTED BUTTER, MELTED

PREHEAT THE BROILER. Cut a razor-thin slice from both ends of the pound cake to reveal the interior. Cut the trimmed loaf of pound cake crosswise into 8 equal slices. Trim each slice to form perfect, uniform, squares. Stir the sugar and cinnamon together in a bowl. Brush both sides of the pound cake slices with the melted butter and sprinkle generously with the cinnamon-sugar. Place the slices on a large baking sheet and broil until the sugar on top starts to bubble and turn brown, 1 to 2 minutes. Remove the baking sheet from the oven, turn the slices over, and broil the second sides in the same way. Transfer the sheet to a wire rack to cool. Use a serrated knife to carefully cut each slice into 4 equal squares.

It is impossible to have a lukewarm response to chocolate. Passion, desire, and giddy delight have swirled in the wake of this glamorous treat since Montezuma gave Cortés his first sip of the original *tchocolatl*, the Aztec ruler's cacao-based, spiced energy drink. The Spanish popularized a warm, sweetened version of this drink in the early 1500s, and chocolate, in all its manifestations, has been hugely popular ever since.

Cacao beans come from tropical evergreen trees and after harvest are fermented, dried, and roasted. The cacao "nibs," the meat of the cacao bean, are then ground and heated to create thick, rich chocolate liquor. Chocolate liquor is the basis of all other chocolates—and that's where the fun begins.

## CHOCOLATE: *A Guide*

### CHOCOLATE CURLS AND CHOCOLATE SHARDS
For quick curls, soften a thick block of chocolate (6 to 8 ounces) in the microwave for about 10 seconds. Scrape a vegetable peeler firmly down one side of the block to form a curl. Place the curls on a plate and refrigerate them until firm enough to handle.

For chocolate shards, line a baking sheet with parchment paper. Spread melted chocolate into a thin layer over the parchment. Allow the chocolate to harden. Peel the chocolate from the parchment and break it into irregular shards. Place the shards on a plate and refrigerate them until they are firm enough to handle.

### COCOA BUTTER
This is the fat extracted from the chocolate liquor. Cocoa butter is the only cacao product in white chocolate.

### COCOA POWDER
The solids that remain from the chocolate liquor after some or most of the cocoa butter has been extracted, dried, and crushed into a fine powder.

### DARK CHOCOLATE
Chocolate manufacturers are very secretive about their methods for blending chocolate liquors made from cacao beans from different regions of the world, from the highly prized Venezuelan beans to the more robust and plentiful beans from Africa and Brazil. Chocolate liquor is blended with sugar, emulsifiers such as lecithin (added to prevent the chocolate from separating), vanilla, and sometimes cocoa butter for additional creaminess. Dark chocolates can contain anywhere from 35 percent chocolate liquor all the way to 82 percent chocolate liquor.

### MELTING CHOCOLATE
Melting chocolate takes patience and a light touch. Chocolate is easier to melt if it has been chopped into small, uniform pieces. You can put the chopped chocolate in a stainless-steel bowl and place the bowl over (but not touching) a pan of barely simmering water, but you must be careful that no steam comes into contact with the melting chocolate. As anyone who works with chocolate knows, a little bit of moisture is the kiss of death to a creamy, melted chocolate. When small amounts of moisture hit the melting chocolate—from steam to water droplets to the misguided addition of a few teaspoons of liqueur—the chocolate will instantly "seize," which means it thickens and hardens into chalky clumps. Once chocolate seizes, it can rarely be remelted. Chocolate needs to be melted completely on its own, or accompanied by a fat such as butter or warm cream, or with a large amount of liquid to prevent it from seizing.

If I need to melt chocolate by itself, I prefer to use the microwave. For this method, I place the chopped chocolate or chocolate chips (no more than 6 to 8 ounces at a time) in a single layer on a large dinner plate (not a bowl). Place the plate, uncovered, in the microwave and heat the chocolate on medium for about 1 minute. Check the chocolate after 1 minute; if it is soft and shiny, stir it on the plate until it is smooth. (Chocolate won't melt into a puddle in the microwave, but will only soften and turn glossy; you will need to stir it.) If the chocolate isn't yet soft enough to stir smooth, continue to heat it in 30-second increments, checking after each session, until it is soft enough to stir smooth.

## MILK CHOCOLATE

To make the familiar and well-loved milk chocolate, chocolate liquor is blended with a high percentage of sugar, milk solids, and vanilla. Sweet and mild, milk chocolate is a favorite of candy makers and children. Milk chocolate is more difficult (but not impossible) to cook and bake with, as it quickly becomes grainy if overheated.

## PLAYING WITH PERCENTAGES

Currently, many manufacturers are listing the percentage of chocolate liquor in their chocolate on the package label. The higher the percentage of chocolate, the less sugar, therefore the less sweet it is. A 70 percent chocolate, for example, has approximately 30 percent sugar and is accordingly more intense than a dark chocolate labeled 62 percent. The chocolate you choose is strictly a matter of taste, and a higher percentage of chocolate liquor shouldn't be seen as a barometer for the quality of the chocolate. A bittersweet 70 percent chocolate may be delicious in a flourless chocolate cake, but may not be sweet enough to be chopped into chunks for a chocolate chip cookie. Chocolates with a higher percentage of chocolate liquor can also be a little more temperamental, and not perform as reliably in your recipes as the lower-percentage chocolate it may have been developed with. Experimenting with chocolates of different percentages from different manufacturers can be fun, so let your taste buds be your guide on this enjoyable journey. A solid, standard semisweet chocolate, such as Ghirardelli, Callebaut, or Hershey's Dark, is 51 to 56 percent chocolate liquor. If you choose chocolates between approximately 56 and 62 percent chocolate liquor, you shouldn't have any problems with performance. There are many quality chocolate makers, including the above mentioned, Scharffen Berger, Guittard, Lindt, and Valrhona. Take your time sampling them all and picking your favorite.

## STORING CHOCOLATE

A little care must be taken to store chocolate and keep it happy. Chocolate is a difficult neighbor; it doesn't like humidity, strong odors, heat, or too much light. Store chocolate in a cool, dark cupboard. For extra protection, keep chocolate in self-sealing plastic bags. Although well-wrapped chocolate can theoretically stay fresh for up to a year, if you are an occasional baker and chocolate isn't something you cook with often, it's best to buy it in small quantities and store it for shorter periods of time.

## TEMPERING CHOCOLATE

Tempering is the delicate process of slowly heating and cooling chocolate so that when it hardens it maintains a crisp consistency and a glossy sheen. Tempering chocolate takes skill, patience, and, most important, lots of practice. To temper 1 pound of chocolate, chop the chocolate into small, uniform pieces and melt half of it, heating it to a temperature of 115° to 120°F (use a candy thermometer to test the temperature), stirring until smooth. Add the remaining chocolate pieces to the melted chocolate and stir until completely smooth and melted, and the chocolate is between 84°F and 88°F.

## UNSWEETENED CHOCOLATE

Simply solid chunks of chocolate liquor with no added sweeteners or flavorings. The robust flavor of unsweetened chocolate is too bitter to eat alone, but is commonly used in highly sweetened recipes such as brownies and many classic American layer cakes.

## WHITE CHOCOLATE

A smooth, very creamy confection made from cocoa butter, sugar, milk, and flavorings such as vanilla. True white chocolate must contain at least 20 percent cocoa butter.

Hot chocolate and churros is a snack beloved thoughout Spain. For the hot chocolate, the thicker and richer, the better. Churros, hot and crisp from the fryer and glittering with cinnamon and sugar, are the traditional accompaniment—perfect for dunking.

# Outrageously Thick Spanish Hot Chocolate with Churros SERVES 6

**FOR THE HOT CHOCOLATE:**

6 CUPS WHOLE MILK

2 TABLESPOONS CORNSTARCH

1/4 CUP DUTCH-PROCESSED COCOA POWDER (I LIKE VALRHONA)

3/4 CUP SUGAR

PINCH OF SALT

1 TEASPOON PURE VANILLA EXTRACT

8 TO 12 OUNCES SEMISWEET CHOCOLATE, CHOPPED

**FOR THE CHURROS:**

1 CUP WATER

1/4 CUP LIGHT OLIVE OIL (NOT EXTRA-VIRGIN)

1/2 TEASPOON SALT

1 1/4 CUPS UNBLEACHED ALL-PURPOSE FLOUR, SIFTED AND THEN MEASURED

4 LARGE EGGS

PEANUT OR CANOLA OIL FOR DEEP-FRYING

1 CUP SUGAR

3 TABLESPOONS GROUND CINNAMON

1 CUP HEAVY CREAM, WHIPPED TO SOFT PEAKS

**TO MAKE THE HOT CHOCOLATE:** Pour 5 1/2 cups of the milk into a large, heavy-bottomed saucepan. In a small bowl or cup, stir together the cornstarch, cocoa powder, sugar, and salt. Add the remaining 1/2 cup milk to form a smooth paste. Heat the milk over medium heat and just before it begins to boil, whisk in the cocoa mixture. Bring to a boil, stirring constantly, and cook for 1 minute, or until the mixture thickens slightly. Remove from the heat and stir in the vanilla and about 8 ounces of the chocolate. Stir until the chocolate is completely melted and combined. Taste the hot chocolate; if desired, stir in 4 more ounces of chocolate (or to taste) for an even richer flavor. Set aside and keep warm.

**TO MAKE THE CHURROS:** Combine the water, olive oil, and salt in a medium heavy-bottomed, nonaluminum saucepan. Bring to a full, rolling boil over high heat. Remove from the heat and add the flour all at once. Stir briskly with a wooden spoon until the dough pulls away from the sides of the pan and gathers in a clump around the spoon. Place the pan over medium heat and stir the batter briskly for 30 to 60 seconds longer. This will dry any excess moisture and eliminate any raw flour taste from the dough.

**LINE A WORK SURFACE WITH A PIECE OF ALUMINUM FOIL AND TURN THE DOUGH OUT ONTO THE FOIL.** Pat the dough into an 8-inch circle and let cool for 5 minutes. Return the dough to the pan. Beat the eggs, one at a time, into the dough, stirring briskly after each addition just until the egg is fully incorporated and the dough smooths out. The final dough should be smooth, slightly sticky, and malleable, but firm enough to form soft peaks and be piped or scooped and hold its shape.

## Sweet Story

During a port call while stationed in the Mediterranean, my husband spent the day with friends at the *feria* in Jerez, Spain. The *feria* is a colorful spring festival that starts with a horse show and continues throughout the day with men and women, dressed in the traditional clothing of Spanish horsemen from the nineteenth century, parading on horseback and in beautiful carriages around the fair. Tents sponsored by local organizations and sherry bodegas showcasing regional sherries are set up as revelers dance to *las Sevillanas*. Tapas and sherry are enjoyed throughout the day. As the sun sets, the air becomes cool and the fairgrounds are ablaze with colorful lighting. My husband found a little booth that was advertising *chocolate de la taza y churros*. The proprietor asked, *"Cuanto?"* for the number in his party. He replied *"Seis,"* and the man pulled a lever on a large hopper set over a vat of hot oil. Thick dough flowed into the hot oil as he counted out loud *"Uno, dos, tres, cuatro, cinco, seis."* The result was a churro in the form of one big spiral. He fished the spiral out of the oil, tossed it in cinnamon and sugar, and placed it on a large plate. Surrounding the plate were six heavy, white porcelain cups filled with thick Castilian hot chocolate, a fabulous elixir as thick as hot pudding—more a dip than a drink. My husband and his companions all sat quietly at a little table enjoying the last few moments of the *feria* while pulling pieces off the churro and dunking it into their cups as the chocolate began to set.

POUR OIL TO A DEPTH OF 3 INCHES INTO A WOK, large cast-iron skillet, Dutch oven, or deep-fryer. Heat the oil to 365°F. Meanwhile, stir together the sugar and cinnamon in a large shallow dish. Fit a large pastry bag with a large star-shaped tip (I like Ateco #846) and pipe strips or coils of dough right into the hot oil. Fry one large spiral or about 4 strips at a time. Fry the dough until golden brown, using tongs to turn the pastries once in the hot oil, approximately 2 minutes per side. Using a wire-mesh skimmer, transfer the hot churros from the oil to a paper towel–lined plate to drain. While still warm, roll the churros in the cinnamon-sugar. Place churros on a baking sheet and keep warm in a 200°F oven.

LET THE OIL RETURN TO 365°F BEFORE REPEATING WITH THE REMAINING BATTER TO PREPARE THE REMAINING CHURROS. When the churros are all fried, gently rewarm the hot chocolate if necessary.

POUR THE HOT CHOCOLATE INTO SIX 1-CUP BOWLS OR CUPS AND TOP EACH WITH A DOLLOP OF THE WHIPPED CREAM. Serve with the churros for dipping.

Deliciously rich and creamy with a faint boozy edge, these chocolate martinis are a wonderful dessert to make a day ahead of time for a fancy dinner party—and they are deceptively easy to prepare. Just make sure you have enough room in your refrigerator to keep the martinis cold before serving. The spirits listed here are definitely a guide—feel free to experiment with other choices that you find complementary. You can top these martinis with a chocolate kiss, a maraschino cherry (dipped halfway in chocolate, if you like), a fresh raspberry, or a chocolate espresso bean.

# Triple-Layer Chocolate Silk Martini SERVES 8

12 OUNCES BITTERSWEET OR SEMISWEET CHOCOLATE, COARSELY CHOPPED

10 OUNCES MILK CHOCOLATE, COARSELY CHOPPED

8 OUNCES WHITE CHOCOLATE, COARSELY CHOPPED

6 CUPS HEAVY CREAM

2 TABLESPOONS RASPBERRY-FLAVORED VODKA OR RASPBERRY LIQUEUR

2 TABLESPOONS CRÈME DE CACAO OR CHOCOLATE LIQUEUR SUCH AS GODIVA

2 TABLESPOONS VANILLA-FLAVORED VODKA

1/2 TEASPOON PURE VANILLA EXTRACT

PLACE EACH TYPE OF CHOCOLATE IN A SEPARATE HEATPROOF BOWL. Bring the cream just to a boil in a large saucepan. Pour 2 cups of the hot cream into each bowl of chocolate. Let the chocolates and cream sit for 1 minute. Add the raspberry-flavored vodka to the dark chocolate cream. Add the crème de cacao to the milk chocolate cream, and add the vanilla-flavored vodka and vanilla extract to the bowl of white chocolate cream.

WHISK THE WHITE CHOCOLATE MIXTURE SMOOTH; next whisk the milk chocolate smooth; and then finally the dark chocolate (this way you can use one whisk without washing it). Let the bowls of chocolate cream come to room temperature, then cover and refrigerate until well chilled, about 2 hours.

USING A HANDHELD ELECTRIC MIXER, beat the chilled bowl of dark chocolate cream at medium speed until soft peaks form. Divide the dark chocolate cream evenly among 6 martini glasses, gently shaking them to level the cream in the glass. If necessary, use the back of a teaspoon to smooth into an even layer. Refrigerate for 10 minutes.

WHILE THE FIRST LAYER IS CHILLING, beat the milk chocolate cream until it, too, holds soft peaks. Remove the martini glasses from the refrigerator and carefully spoon the milk chocolate cream over the dark chocolate cream, dividing it evenly and being careful not to mix the layers. Smooth the milk chocolate layer using the back of a teaspoon. Return the glasses to the refrigerator and chill for another 10 minutes.

BEAT THE WHITE CHOCOLATE CREAM UNTIL SOFT PEAKS FORM. Divide the white chocolate cream among the glasses, smoothing it over the milk chocolate layer and again being careful not to disturb the layers. Very gently shake each glass to level the top of the cream. Refrigerate until ready to serve. (If refrigerated overnight, cover the top of each martini loosely with plastic wrap.)

I think this is the perfect recipe—it's incredibly easy, requiring only one bowl and a wooden spoon, and it delivers big, chunky, crisp-yet-chewy cookies jam-packed with sweet pecans and big chunks of chocolate. The secret to its easy perfection lies in melting the butter first instead of creaming it with the sugar. I melt the butter in my favorite ceramic bowl in the microwave, then add the remaining ingredients, and my cookie dough is ready in less than 5 minutes.

# The Best One-Bowl Chocolate Chunk–Pecan Cookies MAKES 18 LARGE COOKIES

2 CUPS PECAN HALVES

1 CUP (2 STICKS) UNSALTED BUTTER

3/4 CUP FIRMLY PACKED DARK BROWN SUGAR

3/4 CUP GRANULATED SUGAR

1 TEASPOON SALT

2 TEASPOONS PURE VANILLA EXTRACT

2 LARGE EGGS

2 1/4 CUPS BLEACHED ALL-PURPOSE FLOUR

1/2 TEASPOON BAKING SODA

1/4 TEASPOON BAKING POWDER

2 CUPS SEMISWEET CHOCOLATE CHUNKS

PREHEAT THE OVEN TO 350°F. Place the pecans on a large baking sheet and toast in the oven until they are warm and fragrant, 6 to 9 minutes. Transfer to a plate and let cool completely.

PLACE THE BUTTER IN A LARGE MICROWAVE-SAFE BOWL AND MICROWAVE UNCOVERED ON HIGH FOR 1 MINUTE. Remove from the microwave and stir until completely melted. Using a large wooden spoon, stir both sugars into the melted butter. When combined, add the salt, vanilla, and eggs. Stir until smooth. Stir the flour, baking soda, and baking powder into the batter just until incorporated and a soft dough forms. Carefully fold in the chocolate chunks and cooled toasted pecans.

USE A 2-OUNCE SELF-RELEASING ICE-CREAM SCOOP OR A 1/4-CUP MEASURING CUP TO MEASURE OUT THE COOKIE DOUGH. Place the cookie dough balls on a baking sheet and refrigerate until firm, 45 to 60 minutes. Toward the end of the chilling time, return the oven to 350°F.

PLACE THE CHILLED DOUGH BALLS ON PARCHMENT PAPER–LINED BAKING SHEETS. (I find 9 cookies per sheet to be about right to allow for a little spreading and for the cookies to bake evenly.)

BAKE UNTIL THE COOKIES ARE CRISP AND GOLDEN AROUND THE EDGES BUT STILL A LITTLE SOFT IN THE CENTERS WITHOUT BEING GOOEY, 15 to 18 minutes. Transfer the baking sheets to wire racks and let cool slightly. Using a large metal spatula, transfer the cookies from the baking sheets to the wire racks and let cool to room temperature.

STORED IN SELF-SEALING PLASTIC BAGS, these cookies will keep for 2 days at room temperature. They can also be frozen for up to 2 weeks. You can prepare the cookie dough balls and, after they are chilled, store the unbaked cookies in the freezer for up to 1 month. The cookies can be baked straight from the freezer but will take a few minutes longer.

The silky, rich flavor of Italian mascarpone cheese marries well with dark chocolate and makes for a sublime cheesecake, baked up smooth and buttery in little custard cups and eaten with crunchy, sweet, and delightfully edible shortbread spoons! Add a dollop of whipped cream and a few chocolate curls to the tops of these individual cheesecake pots for the perfect dinner-party dessert.

# Chocolate Mascarpone Cheesecake Pots with Shortbread Spoons SERVES 8

1 CUP HEAVY CREAM

4 OUNCES SEMISWEET CHOCOLATE, FINELY CHOPPED

8 OUNCES MASCARPONE CHEESE

¼ CUP SUGAR

3 LARGE EGGS

1 TEASPOON PURE VANILLA EXTRACT

PINCH OF SALT

1 TABLESPOON DARK RUM, BRANDY, OR GRAND MARNIER (OPTIONAL)

BOILING WATER AS NEEDED

SWEETENED WHIPPED CREAM (SEE PAGE 43) AND CHOCOLATE CURLS (SEE PAGE 20) FOR SERVING

SHORTBREAD SPOONS (PAGE 28) FOR SERVING

POSITION A RACK IN THE MIDDLE OF THE OVEN AND PREHEAT TO 325°F.

IN A SAUCEPAN, bring the cream to a simmer over medium heat. Remove the pan from the heat before the cream starts to boil and add the chocolate, stirring constantly until mixture is smooth. Set aside and let cool to room temperature.

IN A LARGE BOWL, whisk together the mascarpone and sugar until smooth. Add the eggs one at a time, whisking well after each addition until the mixture is smooth. Add the vanilla, salt, and rum (if using) and whisk to combine.

POUR THE COOLED CHOCOLATE MIXTURE INTO THE MASCARPONE CHEESE MIXTURE AND WHISK GENTLY UNTIL SMOOTH.

PUT EIGHT 4-OUNCE CUSTARD CUPS, ramekins, or small ovenproof coffee cups in an empty 9-by-13-inch baking pan. Divide the chocolate-cheesecake mixture among the cups.

PUT THE BAKING DISH IN THE OVEN AND THEN CAREFULLY POUR BOILING WATER INTO THE PAN, adding just enough water to reach halfway up the sides of the custard cups. Cover with aluminum foil.

BAKE UNTIL THE TOPS OF THE CHEESECAKES APPEAR SOLID BUT JIGGLE SLIGHTLY WHEN SHAKEN, 30 to 40 minutes. The perfect consistency is a little soft, but not liquid. The cheesecake pots will firm up as they cool. Transfer the pots from the baking pan to a wire rack and let cool to room temperature. Cover each pot with plastic wrap and refrigerate for at least 4 hours or preferably overnight before serving. The cheesecake pots can be prepared up to 2 days before serving.

TOP EACH CHEESECAKE POT WITH A DOLLOP OF WHIPPED CREAM AND A FEW CHOCOLATE CURLS AND SERVE WITH A SHORTBREAD SPOON.

CONTINUED

## Shortbread Spoons MAKES ABOUT 12 SPOONS

There is nothing more fun than these little cookie spoons. I was lucky enough to find a spoon-shaped cookie cutter, but you can also use a small, sharp paring knife to cut these spoons freehand from the rolled-out dough. Use a small spoon (I like the size of infant feeding spoons) on the dough to use as a template. Chill the cutout cookies until very firm and cold—they will hold their shape better as they bake.

1/2 CUP (1 STICK) UNSALTED BUTTER, AT ROOM TEMPERATURE

1 CUP CONFECTIONERS' SUGAR, SIFTED

1 TEASPOON PURE VANILLA EXTRACT

1 CUP UNBLEACHED ALL-PURPOSE FLOUR

1/4 TEASPOON SALT

IN A BOWL, cream together the butter and sugar. Stir in the vanilla. Add the flour and salt and stir together until the mixture forms a soft dough.

PAT THE DOUGH INTO A DISK AND WRAP IN PLASTIC WRAP. Refrigerate for at least 1 hour and up to 1 week.

ON A LIGHTLY FLOURED WORK SURFACE, roll the dough out 1/4 inch thick and cut into 4-inch spoons (see headnote). Place the shortbread spoons on a parchment paper–lined baking sheet and refrigerate until cold and very firm, 45 to 60 minutes.

POSITION A RACK IN THE MIDDLE OF THE OVEN AND PREHEAT TO 300°F. Remove the shortbread spoons from the refrigerator and immediately place in the oven. Bake until the edges of the cookies are a pale, golden brown but the centers are still very pale, 25 to 30 minutes. Transfer the baking sheets to wire racks and let cool slightly. Using a large metal spatula, transfer the cookies from the baking sheets to the wire racks and let cool to room temperature. Store the cookies, tightly covered at room temperature, for up to 3 days, or freeze for up to 2 weeks.

It sounds fancy, French, and scary. But ganache is really one of the simplest, most versatile confections to prepare. It takes nothing more complicated than heavy cream and chopped bittersweet or semisweet chocolate to conjure up this popular French classic. Warm ganache can be poured over a cake to glaze it; chilled and whipped into a light but rich chocolate frosting; or chilled until firm enough to roll into chocolate truffles. Ganache also makes a luscious, gooey sauce for ice cream and is much easier to prepare than hot fudge.

Since ganache is so simple, the quality of the cream and chocolate are very important. The better the chocolate, the better the ganache. More expensive, higher-quality chocolates often contain more cocoa butter, and the "conching," or grinding, of the ingredients is more complete, resulting in a smoother chocolate and thus a smoother ganache. Most important, let your personal taste buds be your guide. If you like the flavor of the chocolate as it melts on your tongue, then you will enjoy the flavor of your ganache as well.

Traditional ganache recipes call for equal parts heavy cream and chocolate, so for 8 ounces of chocolate you will use 1 cup of heavy cream. To make ganache, the chocolate is first chopped into small, uniform pieces and placed in a wide, shallow bowl. Heavy cream is heated just to a boil and is poured over the chocolate, making sure that the chocolate is completely covered. The chocolate and cream sit together while the heat of the cream melts the chocolate. The two are then very gently stirred together until they combine into a smooth, dark sauce.

That's all there is to basic ganache, but sometimes I like to add a little butter and corn syrup. The butter adds richness and the corn syrup adds luster and shine. Two tablespoons butter and 2 tablespoons light corn syrup added to the standard recipe yields a delicious glossy mixture perfect for saucing desserts from ice cream to bread pudding, or pouring over cakes for a shiny glaze.

Although the simple chocolate flavor of plain ganache is delicious on its own, a little shot of spirits adds a zippy boost, and there are many complementary choices. Dark rum, Armagnac, Grand Marnier, Cognac, whiskey, and Kahlúa all deliver a punch of flavor that marries well with the chocolate. If you don't want to add alcohol, try a few drops of pure extracts such as vanilla or peppermint for additional flavor.

Another way to enhance the flavor of your ganache is to first infuse the cream with natural flavors before you pour it over the chocolate. Infusing extracts the elusive qualities of an ingredient and imparts a complex and subtle flavor to the cream and then to the ganache. Cinnamon sticks, fresh ginger, orange zest, vanilla beans, coarsely ground coffee beans, teas such as Earl Grey, and fresh mint or other fresh herbs can all be added to the cream. Bring the cream and your flavoring(s) of choice to boil. Remove the pan from the heat and cover. Allow the herbs or other ingredients to steep until their flavor and aroma has permeated the cream—at least 3o minutes or up to 1 hour. Strain the flavoring agent from the cream before continuing with the ganache.

## GANACHE 1-2-3

## My Favorite Ganache
### MAKES 1 1/2 CUPS

| | |
|---|---|
| 8 OUNCES FINELY CHOPPED SEMISWEET CHOCOLATE | 2 TABLESPOONS UNSALTED BUTTER |
| 1 CUP HEAVY CREAM | 2 TABLESPOONS LIGHT CORN SYRUP |

PLACE THE CHOCOLATE IN A HEATPROOF BOWL. Combine the cream, butter, and corn syrup in a saucepan. Stir over medium-high heat until butter is melted and the corn syrup is combined with the cream. Bring to a boil. Just as the bubbles start to rise, pour the hot cream mixture over the chocolate. Let stand for 1 minute. Stir until smooth and creamy.

I adapted this recipe from one by Hellmann's, increasing the cocoa powder and sugar and reducing the eggs by one. It's easy to assemble and practically foolproof. The batter is rich and deeply chocolatey, and results in bouncy little cakes that don't dissolve into a shower of crumbs with the first bite. You must, must, must try these with the Caramel-Butterscotch Buttercream; its robust, singed-brown sugar flavor perfectly complements the almost black plainness of the cake.

# Chocolate-Mayonnaise Cupcakes with Caramel-Butterscotch Buttercream Frosting

MAKES 24 STANDARD CUPCAKES

2 CUPS BLEACHED ALL-PURPOSE FLOUR

3/4 CUP NATURAL COCOA POWDER (SEE PAGE 45)

1 TEASPOON BAKING SODA

1/4 TEASPOON SALT

2 CUPS SUGAR

2 LARGE EGGS

1 CUP MAYONNAISE (NOT LOW-FAT)

2 TEASPOONS PURE VANILLA EXTRACT

1 1/3 CUPS BOILING WATER

CARAMEL-BUTTERSCOTCH BUTTERCREAM FROSTING (PAGE 32)

POSITION A RACK IN THE MIDDLE OF THE OVEN AND PREHEAT TO 350°F. Line two standard 12-cup muffin tins with paper cupcake liners.

IN A LARGE BOWL, sift together the flour, cocoa powder, baking soda, and salt. Set aside.

IN ANOTHER BOWL, combine the sugar and eggs and beat with an electric mixer set at medium-high speed until light and fluffy, about 2 minutes. Beat in the mayonnaise and vanilla just until combined. Reduce the speed to medium and beat in half of the flour mixture just until combined. Stop the mixer and scrape down the sides of the bowl. Add half of the boiling water and beat at very low speed just until the batter is smooth, 5 to 10 seconds. Add the remaining flour mixture and beat just until combined, 5 to 10 seconds longer. Beat in the remaining water. The batter will be somewhat thin.

DIVIDE THE BATTER AMONG THE PREPARED CUPCAKE CUPS, filling them about two-thirds full. Bake until a wooden skewer inserted into the center of a cupcake comes out clean, 18 to 22 minutes. Transfer to wire racks and let cool completely. When the cupcakes are completely cool, frost them with the Caramel–Butterscotch Buttercream and serve.

CONTINUED

# Caramel-Butterscotch Buttercream Frosting MAKES ABOUT 5 CUPS

### or enough to generously frost one 9-inch three-layer cake or 24 cupcakes

Glossy and buttery, but with the slightly bittersweet, sophisticated edge of both bourbon and caramel sauce to temper its richness, this buttercream is dreamy piled high on any chocolate cake. If you haven't made classic buttercream before, you will be richly rewarded by the lush creaminess and delectable flavor of the real thing. It takes a little time but isn't difficult to make, and a large stand mixer takes away the pain from the formidable amount of egg beating involved here.

**FOR THE CARAMEL SAUCE:**

1 CUP GRANULATED SUGAR

3 TABLESPOONS WATER

1 CUP HEAVY CREAM

**FOR THE BUTTERSCOTCH BUTTERCREAM:**

6 LARGE EGGS

1½ CUPS FIRMLY PACKED DARK BROWN SUGAR

1 TEASPOON PURE VANILLA EXTRACT

¼ TEASPOON SALT

1½ POUNDS (6 STICKS) COLD UNSALTED BUTTER

2 TABLESPOONS BOURBON (SEE PAGE 53)

TO MAKE THE CARAMEL SAUCE: Combine the granulated sugar and water in a medium, heavy-bottomed saucepan over medium heat. Cook, gently swirling the pan occasionally, until the sugar dissolves and starts to change color. Increase the heat to high and boil until the syrup turns a deep amber color, 4 to 5 minutes. Watch carefully, as it can burn quickly.

IMMEDIATELY REMOVE THE PAN FROM THE HEAT AND STIR IN THE CREAM WITH A WOODEN SPOON. Reduce the heat to medium-low and cook, stirring constantly, until the caramel thickens, 3 to 5 minutes. Remove the sauce from the heat and let cool.

WHILE THE SAUCE IS COOLING, PREPARE THE BUTTER CREAM: Combine the eggs and brown sugar in the metal bowl of a standing mixer. (Alternatively, use a metal mixing bowl and a handheld electric mixer, but be prepared for a workout.)

FILL A LARGE SAUTÉ PAN OR FRYING PAN WITH WATER AND BRING TO A SIMMER OVER MEDIUM-HIGH HEAT. Place the mixing bowl in the simmering water and whisk the eggs and sugar constantly until the sugar is completely dissolved and the mixture is thick and fluffy and very hot, 3 to 4 minutes. Use an instant-read thermometer to check the temperature; it should be anywhere between 120° and 140°F.

REMOVE THE BOWL FROM THE SIMMERING WATER AND, using the whisk attachment, beat the eggs at medium-high speed until they are tripled in volume and form soft peaks and the bottom of the bowl is completely cool to the touch, about 10 minutes. Beat in the vanilla and salt.

WHILE THE EGGS ARE MIXING, unwrap the individual sticks of butter and rewrap them loosely in plastic wrap. Pound the butter 5 or 6 times with a rolling pin, or until the butter is soft and malleable but still cool.

WITH THE MIXER SPEED STILL ON MEDIUM-HIGH, add the butter, approximately 2 table-spoons at a time, to the egg mixture, beating in each addition until it is incorpo-rated. When all the butter has been incorporated, slowly dribble in the bourbon. Don't start to panic if the buttercream seems too liquidy or looks curdled as you beat in the butter. It will magically emulsify into a smooth, creamy frosting by the time the last little bit of butter is mixed in. Have faith; it's worth it.

WHEN THE BUTTERCREAM IS SMOOTH AND GLOSSY, turn off the mixer and, using a rubber spatula, fold in ½ cup of the cool caramel sauce. For a stronger flavor, fold in up to ½ cup more caramel sauce.

Although it would be nice to have two separate fondue pots to hold your chocolate fondue, it really isn't necessary. Place two ceramic bowls on a serving platter and surround them with a selection of fresh and dried fruits, pound-cake cubes, homemade marshmallows, shortbread fingers, and madeleines. Right before you are ready to serve, heat the cream and combine it with the chopped chocolates and flavorings. Pour the fondues into their individual bowls and you are good to go. The chocolate fondue will stay warm and liquid long enough for it to be devoured.

# White and Dark Chocolate Fondue SERVES 8 with Coconut Madeleines and Homemade Marshmallows

FRESH STRAWBERRIES

FRESH PINEAPPLE AND BANANA CHUNKS

FRESH OR DRIED FIGS

POUND-CAKE CUBES (PURCHASE A LOAF OR MAKE YOUR OWN AND CUT INTO CUBES; SEE PAGE 37) AND SHORTBREAD FINGERS

COCONUT MADELEINES (PAGE 34)

HOMEMADE MARSHMALLOWS (PAGE 35)

**FOR THE FONDUE:**

10 OUNCES WHITE CHOCOLATE, FINELY CHOPPED

8 OUNCES SEMISWEET CHOCOLATE, FINELY CHOPPED

2 1/2 CUPS HEAVY CREAM

2 TABLESPOONS AMARETTO, GRAND MARNIER, OR KIRSCH

2 TABLESPOONS, DARK RUM, KAHLÚA, OR BOURBON

PUT 2 SERVING BOWLS ON A LARGE PLATTER AND SURROUND THEM WITH THE FRUITS, pound-cake cubes, shortbread fingers, madeleines, and marshmallows. Set aside.

TO MAKE THE FONDUE: Place the chopped white chocolate and semisweet chocolate in 2 separate heatproof bowls. Heat the cream in a saucepan over medium-high heat just until it comes to a boil. Pour 1¼ cups of the hot cream over the white chocolate and 1¼ cups over the dark chocolate. Let the chocolates sit for a minute to soften and then stir until smooth. Stir 2 tablespoons of either amaretto, Grand Marnier, or kirsch into the melted white chocolate. Stir 2 tablespoons of either dark rum, Kahlúa, or bourbon into the dark chocolate.

POUR THE FONDUES INTO THE SEPARATE SERVING BOWLS ON THE PLATTER. Serve immediately.

CONTINUED

# Coconut Madeleines MAKES 24 MADELEINES

If you are a baker who abhors specialty pans, you might soften your stance and include a madeleine pan, a metal pan with twelve small shell-shaped indentations, in your *batterie de cuisine*. I think these dainty scallop-shell cakes add a little romance to the fondue offerings, and the combination of coconut and chocolate is delicious. Madeleines are at their best eaten the day they are baked.

2 LARGE EGGS

2 LARGE EGG WHITES

1/3 CUP GRANULATED SUGAR

1 TEASPOON PURE VANILLA EXTRACT

1 CUP UNBLEACHED ALL-PURPOSE FLOUR

1 CUP CONFECTIONERS' SUGAR, SIFTED

PINCH OF SALT

3/4 CUP (11/2 STICKS) UNSALTED BUTTER, MELTED AND COOLED

3/4 CUP SWEETENED SHREDDED COCONUT

IN A LARGE BOWL, using a large wire whisk, gently beat the eggs, egg whites, granulated sugar, and vanilla together until smooth.

SIFT THE FLOUR, confectioners' sugar, and salt together onto a piece of waxed paper and then fold into the batter. Finally, fold the melted butter and coconut into the batter until completely smooth. The batter should be fairly thin. Cover the bowl with plastic wrap and refrigerate for at least 1 hour or up to 24 hours. After chilling, the batter should be thick and very firm.

POSITION A RACK IN THE MIDDLE OF THE OVEN AND PREHEAT TO 375°F. Spray the molds of a madeleine pan with nonstick cooking spray. Fill each shell mold with about 1 tablespoon of batter. Place the pan on a baking sheet and bake until the madeleines are firm and golden brown with a small hump in the center, 10 to 12 minutes.

TRANSFER THE MADELEINES TO A WIRE RACK, popping them out with the tip of a sharp paring knife, and let cool. Wipe any stray crumbs from the pan with a paper towel and spray lightly, again, with cooking spray. Repeat to bake the remaining batter.

# Homemade Marshmallows

**This recipe is adapted from the simple version in *The Joy of Cooking*. Cut these fluffy marshmallows into big squares perfect for dunking in the warm chocolate fondue.**

1 CUP COLD WATER

3 TABLESPOONS UNFLAVORED GELATIN

2 CUPS GRANULATED SUGAR

3/4 CUP LIGHT CORN SYRUP

1/4 TEASPOON SALT

2 TABLESPOONS PURE VANILLA EXTRACT

CORNSTARCH AND CONFECTIONERS' SUGAR FOR DUSTING

POUR 1/2 CUP OF THE COLD WATER INTO A LARGE MIXING BOWL OR THE BOWL OF A MIXER. Sprinkle the gelatin evenly over the water and allow the gelatin to sit and absorb all the water, 45 to 60 minutes.

IN A LARGE SAUCEPAN, combine the remaining 1/2 cup cold water, the granulated sugar, the corn syrup, and the salt. Heat the mixture over medium heat, stirring occasionally until the sugar dissolves. Increase the heat to high and let the mixture come to a boil. Cook the syrup, without stirring, until it reaches 240°F on a candy thermometer. Do not allow the syrup to go past 244°F or the marshmallows will be rubbery rather than tender. Remove the syrup from the heat and slowly beat it into the dissolved gelatin with an electric mixer set at low speed. Increase the mixer speed to high and continue beating until the mixture is very thick and white but still warm, about 15 minutes. Beat in the vanilla.

GENEROUSLY DUST A 9-BY-13-INCH BAKING PAN WITH CORNSTARCH. Pour the marshmallow mixture into the pan, smooth the top with a spatula, and dust the top liberally with confectioners' sugar. Let the marshmallow stand, uncovered at room temperature, for 8 to 12 hours to firm up. Turn the marshmallow from the pan onto a sheet of parchment paper liberally dusted with confectioners' sugar. Cut into 20 large squares. Dust each square with more confectioners' sugar. Store the marshmallows in a tightly covered container until ready to serve.

These dessert sandwiches are more fun than grilled cheese, and really, just as easy. You can use finely chopped chocolate, as I do here, or you can sandwich slices of pound cake together with very firm ganache (see page 29) or even Nutella, for a yummy change of pace. Any of the pound cake recipes offer a wonderful flavor match.

# Grilled Chocolate Pound-Cake Sandwiches à la Mode SERVES 4

1 LOAF (8½ BY 4½ INCHES) POUND CAKE, HOMEMADE (FACING PAGE OR PAGE 104) OR PURCHASED

1 CUP VERY FINELY CHOPPED SEMISWEET CHOCOLATE

3 TO 4 TABLESPOONS UNSALTED BUTTER

1 PINT PREMIUM-QUALITY VANILLA ICE CREAM

CONFECTIONERS' SUGAR FOR DUSTING (OPTIONAL)

SLICE THE POUND CAKE CROSSWISE INTO EIGHT 1-INCH-THICK PIECES. Divide the chocolate into 4 equal portions and mound over 4 of the pound cake slices. Top each with a second slice of pound cake to form a sandwich. Press gently to seal.

MELT THE UNSALTED BUTTER IN A 12-INCH, nonstick sauté pan or skillet over medium heat and cook until bubbly and starting to brown. Slip the four sandwiches into the butter and cook until their bottoms are golden brown and the chocolate is starting to melt, 1 to 2 minutes. Flip the sandwiches and cook until golden on the second side and the chocolate filling is completely creamy and gooey, about 1 minute longer. Transfer the sandwiches to a cutting board. Let cool slightly, then cut each one in half on the diagonal.

TO SERVE, prop half of each sandwich next to the other half, on individual plates and place a ½-cup scoop of ice cream next to the sandwich. Dust with confectioners' sugar, if desired. Serve immediately.

Most pound cake recipes are full of butter and often include heavy cream, sour cream, or buttermilk for added flavor and richness. But I prefer this recipe, which includes cream cheese in the batter. This cake is tender and moist, with a delicious flavor and a firm texture—perfect on its own, or to make delectable croutons for chocolate soup; cut into batons for dipping into fondue; or layered with custard and cream in a delicious trifle. Take the cream cheese and butter out of the refrigerator the night before you bake this cake and let them come to room temperature—it makes the mixing process nearly effortless.

## My Favorite Cream-Cheese Pound Cake MAKES TWO 8 1/2-BY- 4 1/2-INCH LOAVES

1 1/2 CUPS (3 STICKS) UNSALTED BUTTER, AT ROOM TEMPERATURE

8 OUNCES CREAM CHEESE, AT ROOM TEMPERATURE

3 CUPS SUGAR

1/2 TEASPOON SALT

2 TEASPOONS PURE VANILLA EXTRACT

6 LARGE EGGS, AT ROOM TEMPERATURE

3 CUPS BLEACHED ALL-PURPOSE FLOUR, SIFTED AND THEN MEASURED

1 TEASPOON BAKING POWDER

POSITION A RACK IN THE MIDDLE OF THE OVEN AND PREHEAT TO 325°F. Spray two 8 1/2-by-4 1/2-inch loaf pans with nonstick cooking spray.

BEAT THE BUTTER AND CREAM CHEESE TOGETHER IN A LARGE BOWL WITH AN ELECTRIC MIXER UNTIL SMOOTH AND CREAMY. With the mixer running, gradually add the sugar and continue beating until pale and fluffy. Beat in the salt and vanilla.

ADD THE EGGS TO THE BUTTER MIXTURE ONE AT A TIME, beating well after each addition. Sift the flour again along with the baking powder into the batter and, using a large rubber spatula, fold in until no traces of flour remain and the batter is smooth.

DIVIDE THE BATTER BETWEEN THE TWO PREPARED LOAF PANS. Bake until the tops are golden and slightly cracked, and when a skewer is inserted into the center of the cakes comes out with only a few moist crumbs clinging to it, 60 to 75 minutes. Transfer to a wire rack and let cool in the pans for 10 minutes, then turn the cakes out of the pans and let cool to room temperature on the wire rack before serving.

AT THIS POINT THE CAKES CAN BE WRAPPED WELL IN PLASTIC WRAP AND STORED AT ROOM TEMPERATURE FOR UP TO 3 DAYS OR FROZEN FOR UP TO 1 MONTH.

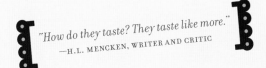

"How do they taste? They taste like more."
—H.L. MENCKEN, WRITER AND CRITIC

**FOR THE GRAHAM CRACKER CRUST:**

3 CUPS CRUSHED GRAHAM CRACKER CRUMBS

1/2 CUP (1 STICK) UNSALTED BUTTER, MELTED

1 TABLESPOON GRANULATED SUGAR

Topped with big loopy swirls of Marshmallow Fluff meringue burnished to a golden bronze, this S'more may be all grown up, but it still knows how to have a good time. A sweet, crumbly graham cracker crust is topped with a dense, very adult, very rich, and very boozy chocolate cream. The combination of liqueurs here is by no means written in stone: dark rum, Grand Marnier, bourbon—just pick two or three complementary flavors as you like and substitute an equal amount for what I have suggested here.

# All-Grown-Up S'mores MAKES 15 S'MORES

**FOR THE CHOCOLATE FILLING:**

8 LARGE EGG YOLKS

1 1/2 CUPS CONFECTIONERS' SUGAR, SIFTED

2 TABLESPOONS COGNAC OR BRANDY

2 TABLESPOONS WHITE CRÈME DE CACAO

2 TABLESPOONS KAHLÚA

1 TEASPOON PURE VANILLA EXTRACT

1/8 TEASPOON SALT

1 CUP (2 STICKS) UNSALTED BUTTER

2 TABLESPOONS DUTCH-PROCESSED COCOA POWDER (SEE PAGE 45)

12 OUNCES SEMISWEET OR BITTER-SWEET CHOCOLATE, FINELY CHOPPED

1 1/2 CUPS HEAVY CREAM, WHIPPED TO SOFT PEAKS

**FOR THE MARSHMALLOW FLUFF MERINGUE:**

3 LARGE EGG WHITES

PINCH OF SALT

PINCH OF CREAM OF TARTAR

1/4 TEASPOON PURE VANILLA EXTRACT

1 CUP MARSHMALLOW FLUFF

PREHEAT THE OVEN TO 350°F.

TO MAKE THE CRUST: Combine the graham cracker crumbs with the melted butter and granulated sugar until well combined. Press into the bottom of a 9-by-13-inch metal baking pan. Bake the crust until starts to brown and become crisp, about 10 minutes. Transfer to a wire rack and let cool completely.

TO MAKE THE FILLING: Using an electric mixer, beat the egg yolks and confectioners' sugar together in a large bowl until they are thick and the color of butter. Beat in the Cognac, crème de cacao, Kahlúa, vanilla, and salt.

MELT THE BUTTER IN A MEDIUM SAUCEPAN OVER LOW HEAT AND WHISK IN COCOA POWDER UNTIL SMOOTH. Remove the pan from the heat, add the chocolate, and stir until the chocolate is melted and the mixture is smooth. Let cool slightly, then gradually beat into the egg mixture.

FOLD THE SOFTLY BEATEN HEAVY CREAM INTO THE CHOCOLATE MIXTURE JUST UNTIL COMBINED. Spoon the chocolate cream over the graham cracker crust, smoothing it evenly with a spatula. Cover the pan with plastic wrap and refrigerate until very firm, at least 4 hours or up to overnight.

WHEN READY TO SERVE, MAKE THE MERINGUE: Using an electric mixer set at low speed, beat the egg whites until foamy. Add the salt and cream of tartar and beat at medium speed until soft peaks form. Beat in the vanilla. Add the Marshmallow Fluff to the egg whites a little at a time, beating constantly until stiff peaks form.

CAREFULLY CUT THE S'MORES INTO 15 LARGE SQUARES. Place each S'more on a dessert plate. Top each with 1/2 cup of the meringue in a large dollop. Use a small kitchen torch to carefully burnish the meringue until tipped with golden brown. Serve immediately.

Every year I know Christmas is coming when I find my mailbox brimming with fancy food catalogs, their pages splashed with photos of exotic treats. I'm truly dazzled by the extravagant cakes: towering layers filled with ganache and cream, doused with coconut, or wrapped in colorful fondant or marzipan, sporting spun-sugar flowers and ribbons. Inspired by their stunningly expensive glamour, this recipe evolved from a simple chocolate soufflé cake to one bathed in a shimmering cloak of nutty caramel—minus the spun-sugar bow.

# Chocolate Caramel-Pecan Soufflé Cake
### SERVES 10 TO 12

**FOR THE CAKE:**

1 CUP (2 STICKS) UNSALTED BUTTER, CUT INTO TABLESPOONS, PLUS EXTRA, MELTED, FOR BRUSHING

1 CUP SUPERFINE SUGAR, PLUS EXTRA FOR SPRINKLING

1 POUND BITTERSWEET OR SEMISWEET CHOCOLATE, FINELY CHOPPED

8 LARGE EGGS, SEPARATED, AT ROOM TEMPERATURE

1/4 TEASPOON SALT

2 TABLESPOONS BOURBON (SEE PAGE 53)

1 TEASPOON PURE VANILLA EXTRACT

1/2 TEASPOON CREAM OF TARTAR

**FOR THE CARAMEL-PECAN SAUCE:**

1 CUP GRANULATED SUGAR

3 TABLESPOONS WATER

PINCH OF CREAM OF TARTAR

1 CUP PECAN HALVES

3/4 CUP HEAVY CREAM

1/4 TEASPOON SALT

2 TABLESPOONS BOURBON (SEE PAGE 53)

SWEETENED WHIPPED CREAM (PAGE 43) OR VANILLA ICE CREAM FOR SERVING (OPTIONAL)

**POSITION A RACK IN THE MIDDLE OF THE OVEN AND PREHEAT TO 350°F.** Brush a 10-inch springform pan with melted butter, and coat the bottom and sides of the pan with superfine sugar. Tap out any excess sugar.

**TO MAKE THE CAKE:** Combine the chocolate and 1 cup butter in a microwave-safe bowl. Microwave, uncovered, on medium until the butter is melted and the chocolate becomes soft and shiny, 1 1/2 to 4 minutes. Remove from the micro-wave after 1 1/2 minutes and stir; if the chocolate is not completely melted, continue to microwave as needed for 30-second intervals, stirring between intervals, until melted, smooth and thoroughly combined with the butter. Set aside.

**IN A LARGE BOWL,** using an electric mixer set at medium speed, beat the egg yolks and salt until smooth. Gradually add 1/2 cup of the superfine sugar to the egg yolks, beating until the mixture is thick and pale yellow and forms a slowly dissolving ribbon on the surface of the batter when the beaters are lifted, 4 to 6 minutes. Whisk in the bourbon and vanilla. Gradually whisk the egg mixture into the melted chocolate and butter.

**IN A LARGE,** clean, stainless-steel bowl, beat the egg whites and the cream of tartar with an electric mixer set at low speed until foamy. Increase the mixer speed to high and continue beating until the egg whites form soft peaks. Keep beating, adding the remaining 1/2 cup superfine sugar 1 tablespoon at a time, until stiff peaks form.

**STIR ONE-THIRD OF THE EGG WHITES INTO THE CHOCOLATE BATTER TO LIGHTEN IT.** Using a rubber spatula, carefully fold the remaining egg whites into the chocolate batter just until blended.

CONTINUED

> *"Clearly, it is not the lovelorn sufferer who seeks solace in chocolate, but rather the chocolate-deprived individual who, desperate, seeks in mere love a pale approximation of bittersweet euphoria."*
> — FROM CHOCOLATE: THE CONSUMING PASSION, BY SANDRA BOYNTON

CONTINUED

SPOON THE BATTER INTO THE PREPARED PAN. Bake until the cake rises and appears puffy and firm, 25 to 30 minutes. The cake should still be moist, but not liquid, in the center, so a wooden skewer inserted into the center of the cake should not come out clean, but with very moist crumbs clinging to it.

MEANWHILE, MAKE THE TOPPING: Combine the granulated sugar, water, and cream of tartar in a large, heavy saucepan. Cook, gently swirling the pan occasionally, over medium heat until the sugar dissolves and starts to turn color. Increase the heat to high and boil until the syrup turns a deep amber color, 4 to 5 minutes. Watch carefully, as it can burn quickly.

IMMEDIATELY REMOVE THE PAN FROM THE HEAT AND STIR IN THE NUTS, then the cream and salt. Use a long-handled wooden spoon to carefully stir in the cream, as the caramel has a tendency to hiss and splash as the cold cream hits it. Place the pan over low heat and cook, stirring constantly, until the caramel thickens, 3 to 4 minutes. Remove from the heat and stir in the bourbon. Set aside and keep warm.

REMOVE THE CAKE FROM THE OVEN AND LET COOL ON A WIRE RACK FOR 15 MINUTES. The cake will fall slightly as it cools. Remove the sides of the pan. Spoon the warm caramel-pecan topping over the top of the cake and allow the cake and topping to cool completely at room temperature before serving.

USE A LONG, sharp knife dipped in boiling water and wiped dry to cut the cake. Dip knife in boiling water and wipe clean for each slice. Serve slices of cake nestled next to a dollop of sweetened whipped cream or fat scoop of vanilla ice cream, if desired.

Almost any dessert tastes better with a big spoonful of whipped cream to top it off. Here are some tips for mastering the perfect dollop.

### USE HEAVY CREAM

I like to use heavy cream instead of whipping cream, as it has a slightly higher percentage of butterfat, yielding a richer and more stable whipped cream. When whipped, cream will double in volume—therefore 1 cup of cream will yield 2 cups whipped cream.

### CHILL THE BOWL

Chilling the mixing bowl and the beaters in the freezer for 15 minutes shortens the amount of time it takes to whip the cream.

### WHIP TO SOFT PEAKS

As an accompaniment, cream is best whipped to soft peaks. Cream whipped to the "soft peak" stage will be very thick and have lots of body. The cream will be thick enough to form well-defined peaks that slowly droop over themselves when the beaters are lifted.

### SWEETEN TO TASTE

I like to sweeten my whipped cream before I dollop it on top of my desserts, but you don't need a lot of sugar to do it. In general, 2 or 3 tablespoons of sugar per cup of cream is plenty. To see if this is sweet enough for you, stir the sugar and cream together before you whip it, and taste for sweetness. Feel free to add more sugar, 1 tablespoon at a time, until it is just right for your tastebuds.

### SUGAR, SUGAR

You can use either granulated sugar or confectioners' sugar to sweeten your cream. Confectioners' sugar contains a touch of cornstarch, so cream sweetened with it will hold its shape a little longer before collapsing; it is the sweetener to choose if you want to refrigerate your whipped cream for awhile before serving.

### ADD A TOUCH OF FLAVOR

A few drops of vanilla extract gives a lovely flavor and fragrance to whipped cream without overwhelming the dessert it will be topping. Try ½ to 1 teaspoon vanilla per cup of heavy cream.

## WHIPPED CREAM

# Sweetened Whipped Cream

MAKES 2 CUPS

1 CUP HEAVY CREAM

2 TO 3 TABLESPOONS GRANULATED OR CONFECTIONERS' SUGAR

1 TEASPOON PURE VANILLA EXTRACT

PLACE A MIXING BOWL AND MIXER BEATERS IN THE FREEZER FOR 15 MINUTES. Combine all the ingredients in the bowl and beat, using an electric mixer set at medium-low speed, until the cream starts to thicken. Increase the speed to medium and continue beating until the cream nearly doubles in volume and forms soft peaks.

I love cupcakes. I was a fan long before Magnolia Bakery in New York, Sprinkles in Los Angeles, and Cupcake Royale in Seattle made them the iconic dessert of the new millennium. I think they possess powers no love potion can match. I met Jim O'Connor, a navy lieutenant, twenty years ago in a San Francisco bar, Pat O'Shea's Mad Hatter, where the sign out front reads, "We cheat tourists and drunks." After two dates, Jim left for San Diego to spend six weeks there preparing for engineering exams. I sat with my roommate Jackie, in our little apartment kitchen in the Richmond District, thumbing through an old *Chocolatier* magazine trying to come up with something delicious to bake and mail to him. Black Bottom Cupcakes are fun and easy, with a darkly moist, slightly bittersweet crumb and a gooey, chocolate chip–studded, cheesecake-like center. I wrapped each little cake individually and sent them off to San Diego. We were engaged two weeks after he returned to San Francisco. I'd like to think it was my winning charm, or stunning beauty, but I'm pretty sure it was the cupcakes.

**FOR THE FILLING:**

8 OUNCES MASCARPONE CHEESE

1/2 CUP CONFECTIONERS' SUGAR

1 LARGE EGG

PINCH OF SALT

1 TEASPOON PURE VANILLA EXTRACT

1 CUP MINIATURE SEMISWEET CHOCOLATE CHIPS

# Black Bottom Cupcakes MAKES 24 STANDARD CUPCAKES

**FOR THE CAKE BATTER:**

1 1/2 CUPS BLEACHED ALL-PURPOSE FLOUR

1/2 CUP FIRMLY PACKED DARK BROWN SUGAR

1/2 CUP GRANULATED SUGAR

1/4 CUP NATURAL COCOA POWDER (SEE FACING PAGE)

1 TEASPOON BAKING SODA

1/4 TEASPOON SALT

1 CUP BOILING WATER

1/3 CUP VEGETABLE OIL

1 TABLESPOON APPLE CIDER VINEGAR

1 TEASPOON PURE VANILLA EXTRACT

**FOR THE CHOCOLATE GLAZE:**

8 OUNCES SEMISWEET CHOCOLATE, FINELY CHOPPED

3/4 CUP (1 1/2 STICKS) UNSALTED BUTTER, CUT INTO 6 PIECES

1/4 CUP LIGHT CORN SYRUP

1 TEASPOON PURE VANILLA EXTRACT

PREHEAT THE OVEN TO 350°F. Line two standard 12-cup cupcake tins with paper cupcake liners.

TO MAKE THE FILLING: In a medium bowl, cream together the mascarpone, confectioners' sugar, egg, salt, and vanilla until smooth and creamy. Stir in the chocolate chips.

TO MAKE THE CAKE BATTER: In a large bowl, whisk together the flour, brown sugar, granulated sugar, cocoa powder, baking soda, and salt. In a 2-cup measuring cup, combine the boiling water, oil, vinegar, and vanilla. Make a well in the center of the dry ingredients and pour in the liquid ingredients. Stir together until smooth.

FILL EACH CUPCAKE CUP ONE-FOURTH FULL OF BATTER AND TOP WITH A HEAPING TABLESPOON OR SO OF THE FILLING; divide it evenly and use it all. Top the filling with the remaining batter, dividing it evenly. Bake until cupcakes are puffed and firm, about 25 to 28 minutes.

MEANWHILE, MAKE THE GLAZE: Combine all the ingredients in a microwave-safe bowl and microwave on high for 1 minute. Remove from the microwave and stir until smooth. If the chocolate is not completely melted, continue to microwave for 30-second intervals and stir until smooth.

TRANSFER THE CUPCAKES IN THE PANS TO A WIRE RACK AND LET COOL COMPLETELY. When cool, dip the top of each cupcakes in the chocolate glaze (feel free to double dip, if you like!). Let the excess glaze drip from the cupcakes for a few seconds and then place the cupcake right-side up on the wire rack until the glaze firms up before serving.

Cocoa powder shouldn't be considered second best to dark chocolate when you are thinking of creating a rich chocolate dessert. In fact, cocoa is often the better choice due to its intense, concentrated flavor.

There are two types of cocoa powder widely available to bakers today: natural and Dutch-processed, or alkalized, cocoa. Although different, they both deserve a place on your pantry shelves. More and more chocolate manufacturers are adding cocoa powders to their list of chocolate products. Hershey's, Bensdorp, Droste, Scharffen Berger, Valrhona, Callebaut, and Merckens are all fine choices.

### AU NATUREL

Natural, or nonalkalized, cocoa powder is the traditional cocoa familiar to most American bakers in Hershey's square, brown box. Natural cocoa is very bitter and naturally acidic with a pale, dusky brown color and a hearty flavor. Natural cocoa is the best choice for classic American cakes, brownies, and other desserts made with lots of sugar, often leavened with baking soda. Most important of all, natural cocoa performs best in dishes that need to be cooked or baked. Natural cocoa powder is usually sifted together with the flour and other dry ingredients, or it can be dissolved in a little hot liquid to make the flavor "bloom" before it is added to the rest of the ingredients. The powerful flavor of natural cocoa is particularly delicious in cake recipes that include sour cream, buttermilk, and brown sugar.

### GOING DUTCH

A nineteenth-century Dutchman named Coenraad J. van Houten developed a process to balance the naturally occurring acidity in cocoa beans. Before shelling and grinding them, he soaked the cocoa nibs in an alkaline (low-acid) solution, thereby tempering the natural bitterness of the cocoa bean. Modulating the acidity seems to enrich and enhance the chocolate flavor and the dark color of the cocoa. This deep, rich mellowness makes Dutch-processed cocoa the perfect choice in recipes where cocoa grabs the spotlight. It is the perfect choice when brewing up a cup of hot chocolate, for coating chocolate truffles, making a frozen chocolate sorbet, or sprinkling over desserts as a garnish. For traditional European desserts that are leavened only with beaten eggs or egg whites, Dutch-processed cocoa powder really shines. If a recipe calls for baking powder as a leavening agent, then Dutch-processed cocoa can also be used. Don't try and substitute one type of cocoa for the other. Using Dutch-processed cocoa in a cake leavened with baking soda, without any other acidic ingredients to balance it, will make the batter too alkaline—the cake won't rise properly and it may have a disagreeable flat, soapy flavor.

**A TALE OF TWO COCOAS**

I got my first paying job as a cook the summer after my sophomore year in college, when I became the lunch cook at Mountain Meadow Ranch, a rustic mountain retreat owned and run by a group of family friends in the Trinity Alps of California. Along with preparing lunch, I was also responsible for desserts. Vicki Villarreal, our very laid-back, very trusting kitchen manager, gave me lots of freedom to be creative and try new recipes, but one of everyone's favorites was a recipe Vicki handed down for this classic, very simple, chocolate cake. I've modified it slightly, but the intense chocolate flavor is the same.

# Mountain Meadow Chocolate Fudge Cake SERVES 15

2 CUPS ALL-PURPOSE FLOUR

1 TEASPOON BAKING POWDER

1/4 TEASPOON BAKING SODA

1/4 TEASPOON SALT

1 CUP (2 STICKS) UNSALTED BUTTER

1 CUP BOILING WATER

4 OUNCES UNSWEETENED CHOCOLATE, CHOPPED

2 CUPS SUGAR

1/2 CUP BUTTERMILK

2 LARGE EGGS

1 TABLESPOON PURE VANILLA EXTRACT

**FOR THE FUDGE-PECAN ICING:**

3 OUNCES UNSWEETENED CHOCOLATE, COARSELY CHOPPED

1/2 CUP (1 STICK) UNSALTED BUTTER

1/3 CUP BUTTERMILK

1 TEASPOON PURE VANILLA EXTRACT

PINCH OF SALT

3 TO 4 CUPS CONFECTIONERS' SUGAR, SIFTED

1 1/2 CUPS CHOPPED PECANS, TOASTED (SEE PAGE 89)

POSITION A RACK IN THE MIDDLE OF THE OVEN AND PREHEAT TO 400°F. Brush a 9-by-13-inch baking pan with melted butter or spray with a nonstick cooking spray.

SIFT THE FLOUR, baking powder, baking soda, and salt together into a large bowl and set aside.

COMBINE THE BUTTER, boiling water, and chocolate in a saucepan. Place the saucepan over medium-low heat, and whisk gently until the butter and chocolate are melted and the mixture is smooth. Remove the pan from the heat and whisk in the sugar. Quickly whisk in the buttermilk and then the eggs and vanilla. Using an electric mixer set at medium speed, beat the chocolate mixture into the dry ingredients just until combined and a smooth batter forms, about 1 minute.

POUR THE BATTER IMMEDIATELY INTO THE PREPARED PAN. Bake until the cake starts to pull away from the sides of the pan and a wooden skewer inserted into the middle of the cake comes out clean, 20 to 25 minutes.

MEANWHILE, MAKE THE ICING: Combine the chocolate, butter, and buttermilk in a saucepan and cook, stirring over medium heat, until the chocolate is melted. Remove from the heat and whisk in the vanilla, salt, and 3 cups of the sifted confectioners' sugar. If you would like the icing sweeter and thicker, whisk in the remaining confectioners' sugar to taste. Stir in the pecans.

TRANSFER THE CAKE TO A WIRE RACK AND POUR THE WARM ICING OVER THE CAKE WHILE IT, too, is still warm in the pan. Let cool completely, then cut into squares and serve.

A cross between a cookie and a brownie, these chocolate-stuffed cookies are rich and delicious. For this cookie, feel free to chop up your favorite semisweet or bittersweet chocolate, or use chocolate chunks made especially for baking. Sandwich two big cookies with the deepest, darkest, deadliest chocolate-fudge ice cream you can find—the perfect answer to all your chocolate dessert emergencies. You can scoop the ice cream in advance and store the scoops, well wrapped, in the freezer so they are ready to go when you want to make your sandwiches. The cookies will keep, stored separately in a tightly covered container, for up to 3 days, or frozen for up 1 month (make sure to let them thaw before sandwiching with ice cream).

# Sticky Fingers Triple-Chocolate Ice-Cream Sandwiches MAKES 12 ICE-CREAM SANDWICHES

**FOR THE TRIPLE-CHOCOLATE COOKIES:**

12 OUNCES SEMISWEET CHOCOLATE, FINELY CHOPPED

1 OUNCE UNSWEETENED CHOCOLATE, FINELY CHOPPED

1/2 CUP (1 STICK) UNSALTED BUTTER

4 LARGE EGGS

1 CUP FIRMLY PACKED LIGHT BROWN SUGAR

1 CUP GRANULATED SUGAR

2 TEASPOONS PURE VANILLA EXTRACT

1 1/4 CUPS BLEACHED ALL-PURPOSE FLOUR

3/4 TEASPOON BAKING POWDER

1/2 TEASPOON SALT

1 1/2 CUPS MILK CHOCOLATE CHUNKS

1 1/2 CUPS SEMISWEET CHOCOLATE CHUNKS

1 1/2 QUARTS PREMIUM DARK CHOCOLATE-FUDGE, CHOCOLATE BROWNIE, CHOCOLATE-CHOCOLATE CHIP, OR VANILLA ICE CREAM, SOFTENED

CONFECTIONERS' SUGAR FOR SPRINKLING (OPTIONAL)

POSITION A RACK IN THE MIDDLE OF THE OVEN AND PREHEAT TO 350°F. Line 2 baking sheets with parchment paper and spray lightly with nonstick cooking spray.

TO MAKE THE COOKIES: Combine the semisweet chocolate, unsweetened chocolate, and butter in a microwave-safe bowl. Microwave, uncovered, on high for 1 minute. Remove from the microwave and stir until completely melted. If the mixture is not completely melted, continue to microwave for 30-second intervals, and stir until smooth.

IN A BOWL, beat together the eggs, sugars, and vanilla with an electric mixer set at medium speed until fluffy. Reduce mixer speed to low and beat in the melted chocolate mixture. Sift in the flour, baking powder, and salt and stir just until combined. Stir in the chocolate chunks.

DROP THE BATTER INTO 24 DOLLOPS (ABOUT 1/4 CUP EACH) ONTO THE BAKING SHEETS AT LEAST 3 INCHES APART. Bake, 1 sheet at a time, until the cookies are firm and have a glossy, crackled exterior similar to a brownie but are still moist inside, 12 to 15 minutes. Remove from the oven and let cool completely on the baking sheets.

WHEN THE COOKIES ARE COMPLETELY COOL, SANDWICH WITH THE ICE CREAM. Gently spread a 1/2-cup scoop of softened ice cream onto the flat side of a cookie. Top with a second cookie, flat-side down, and press together gently. Store the finished sandwiches in the freezer while you continue with the remaining cookies and ice cream. Serve immediately, sprinkled with confectioners' sugar if desired.

Pavlova, a heavenly meringue dessert, is famous for its lush, marshmallowy interior contrasted with a crisp, crunchy outer shell. I love to use rich, almost black, Valrhona cocoa powder to give this ethereal dessert a lovely chocolate punch. Adding malted milk powder to the creamy chocolate filling and topping it with a shower of chopped malted milk balls will lure both children and adults quickly to the table. For a true chocolate experience, drizzle everyone's slice with a little of My Favorite Ganache. The contrasting textures and temperatures of chocolate make every bite a little bit of heaven.

# Chocolate Malted Madness SERVES 8

**FOR THE CHOCOLATE MALTED CREAM:**

1 1/2 CUPS HEAVY CREAM

1/4 CUP MALTED MILK POWDER

6 OUNCES SEMISWEET CHOCOLATE, FINELY CHOPPED

1/2 TEASPOON PURE VANILLA EXTRACT

**FOR THE CHOCOLATE PAVLOVA:**

5 TEASPOONS CORNSTARCH, PLUS EXTRA FOR SPRINKLING

3 TABLESPOONS DUTCH-PROCESSED COCOA POWDER (SEE PAGE 45)

5 LARGE EGG WHITES, AT ROOM TEMPERATURE

1/4 TEASPOON CREAM OF TARTAR

PINCH OF SALT

1 2/3 CUPS SUPERFINE SUGAR

2 TEASPOONS DISTILLED WHITE VINEGAR OR CIDER VINEGAR

1 TEASPOON PURE VANILLA EXTRACT

1 CUP MALTED MILK BALLS, SOME CRACKED IN HALF OR IN PIECES AND SOME LEFT WHOLE

MY FAVORITE GANACHE (PAGE 29)

**TO MAKE THE CHOCOLATE CREAM:** In a large, heavy-bottomed saucepan, heat the cream just until it boils. Remove the saucepan from the heat, stir in the malted milk powder, and sprinkle the chocolate on top. Let stand for 1 minute to soften the chocolate, then stir until smooth. Stir in the vanilla. Refrigerate the chocolate cream until very cold, about 2 hours, stirring once or twice. The mixture should be cold enough to whip, but not so cold that it becomes stiff. If the cream should become too stiff, you can reheat it to soften and chill again to the proper consistency.

**WHILE THE CHOCOLATE CREAM IS CHILLING, MAKE THE PAVLOVA:** Position a rack in the middle of the oven and place a pan of warm water on the bottom shelf of the oven. Preheat the oven to 300°F. Line a flat baking sheet (not an air-cushioned baking sheet) with parchment paper and sprinkle with a little cornstarch.

SIFT TOGETHER THE COCOA POWDER AND 5 TEASPOONS CORNSTARCH INTO A BOWL AND SET ASIDE.

RINSE THE METAL BOWL OF A STAND MIXER WITH WARM WATER AND DRY COMPLETELY. Add the egg whites, cream of tartar, and salt to the warm bowl and beat, using the whisk attachment, until soft peaks form. Add the sugar slowly to the egg whites, 1 tablespoon at a time, beating until completely incorporated. While the mixer is still running, add the cocoa mixture. Stop the mixer and scrape down the sides of the bowl if necessary. Continue beating until cocoa mixture is thoroughly incorporated. Add the vinegar and vanilla and beat for 1 more minute. The mixture should be stiff and glossy.

USE A RUBBER SPATULA TO SPOON THE MERINGUE ON TO THE PREPARED BAKING SHEET AND SPREAD INTO A FAT, 8-inch round. Make a shallow well in the center of the meringue, building up the sides slightly. The meringue should resemble a loose, fluffy (slightly dark and stormy) cloud.

PLACE THE MERINGUE ON THE MIDDLE RACK OF THE OVEN AND IMMEDIATELY REDUCE THE OVEN TEMPERATURE TO 250°F. Bake, without peeking, for 45 minutes, then peek; the meringue should be starting to crisp and look dry. Continue baking another 40 to 45 minutes longer. Turn the oven off and prop the oven door open a crack with the handle of a wooden spoon. Let cool in the oven for an additional 30 minutes. The meringue should be high and fluffy, but the sides may crack slightly—no need to worry.

TRANSFER TO A WIRE RACK TO COOL COMPLETELY. Carefully peel the meringue from the parchment paper and place on a serving platter. Beat the chilled chocolate malted cream just until it forms soft peaks and is a spoonable consistency (overbeating will make the cream grainy). No more than 1 hour before serving, fill the center of the Pavlova with the cold, whipped chocolate cream and top with the cracked and whole malted milk balls. Cut into 8 wedges and serve with the ganache.

This recipe makes a big batch of brownie cups, perfect for creating sundaes. I love having a big bag of these stored in the freezer for last-minute desserts or special after-school snacks. These brownies are free of extra nuts, chocolate chips, or other chunky candy additions, highlighting their simple, rich chocolate flavor. Brushing the muffin tins with melted butter and sprinkling them with a liberal dose of granulated sugar makes these delicate cakes easier to remove and gives them a sparkling, crackly exterior—a lovely contrast to their moist, creamy center. For the sundaes, I usually use one pint of ice cream for every 3 to 4 sundaes, so everyone gets a nice big scoop.

# Sugar-Crusted Brownie Sundaes with Whiskey-Walnut Caramel Sauce

MAKES 22 BROWNIE SUNDAES

1 POUND (4 STICKS) UNSALTED BUTTER, PLUS EXTRA FOR THE MUFFIN TINS

2 CUPS SUGAR, PLUS EXTRA FOR THE MUFFIN TINS

12 OUNCES SEMISWEET CHOCOLATE, CUT INTO SMALL PIECES

6 OUNCES UNSWEETENED CHOCOLATE

6 LARGE EGGS

2 TABLESPOONS PURE VANILLA EXTRACT

1 CUP UNBLEACHED ALL-PURPOSE FLOUR

2 TEASPOONS BAKING POWDER

1 TEASPOON SALT

ABOUT 11/2 QUARTS PREMIUM VANILLA ICE CREAM

WHISKEY-WALNUT CARAMEL SAUCE (PAGE 52)

CONFECTIONERS' SUGAR FOR DUSTING

BRUSH ALL BUT 2 OF THE CUPS OF TWO STANDARD 12-CUP MUFFIN TINS WITH MELTED BUTTER. Spoon about 1 tablespoon of sugar into the greased cups and shake and tap around to cover the bottom and sides of the cups completely with a thick coat of sugar. Tap out any excess sugar.

POSITION A RACK IN THE MIDDLE OF THE OVEN AND PREHEAT TO 350°F.

COMBINE THE BUTTER, semisweet chocolate, and unsweetened chocolate together in a microwave-safe bowl and microwave on high for 2 minutes. Remove from the microwave and stir until completely melted. If the chocolate is not completely melted, continue to microwave for 30-second intervals and stir until smooth.

IN A LARGE BOWL, gently whisk together the eggs, 2 cups sugar, and vanilla just until combined. Stir the chocolate mixture into the egg mixture just until combined. Let cool slightly. Sift the flour, baking powder, and salt over the chocolate mixture and fold in just until combined.

SPOON ABOUT 1/4 CUP OF THE BATTER INTO EACH OF THE PREPARED MUFFIN CUPS. (If you run out of batter before you fill all the cups, make sure to wipe out the butter and sugar of any empty cups before baking the brownies, as otherwise they will melt and burn and, in general, make a huge mess.)

BAKE UNTIL THE TOPS OF THE BROWNIES ARE FIRM AND A TOOTHPICK INSERTED INTO THE CENTER OF A BROWNIE CUP COMES OUT WITH A FEW MOIST CRUMBS CLINGING TO IT, 20 to 25 minutes. Be careful not to overbake. Transfer to a wire rack and let cool.

51

CONTINUED

WHEN THE PANS ARE COOL ENOUGH TO HANDLE, run a thin, sharp knife around the edge of one brownie, then carefully tip it out and catch in your hand. (this will prevent it from cracking and falling apart.) Place the brownie on the wire rack to finish cooling. Continue releasing the brownies, one at a time, from the pans. You can serve the brownie sundaes at this point when they are barely warm, or later when the brownies are completely cool. If you want to save the brownies for another time, make sure they are completely cool before storing in a self-sealing plastic bag or tightly covered container and refrigerating for up to three days or freezing for up to 2 weeks.

TO ASSEMBLE THE SUNDAES, place the brownie cups on individual serving plates and top each with a scoop of vanilla ice cream. Drizzle 1/4 to 1/3 cup of the warm Whiskey-Walnut Caramel Sauce over the ice cream. Dust the sundaes with confectioners' sugar and serve immediately.

## Whiskey-Walnut Caramel Sauce MAKES 2 CUPS

Sweet and delectable, but with a smoky bite, this caramel sauce is perfect over ice cream, or sandwiched between shortbread cookies or florentines, or drizzled over a plain chocolate cake or pound cake. This recipe contains a rather large amount of whiskey and will have a stronger flavor immediately after it is made.

2 CUPS GRANULATED SUGAR

1/2 CUP WHISKEY (SEE FACING PAGE)

1 TEASPOON FRESH LEMON JUICE

2 CUPS HEAVY CREAM

1/2 TEASPOON SALT

1 TABLESPOON PURE VANILLA EXTRACT

1 CUP CHOPPED WALNUTS

COMBINE THE SUGAR, whiskey, and lemon juice in a heavy-bottomed saucepan over medium heat. Cook, gently swirling the pan occasionally, until the sugar dissolves and starts to turn color. Increase the heat to high and boil until the syrup turns a deep amber color, 4 to 5 minutes. Watch carefully, as it can burn quickly.

IMMEDIATELY REMOVE THE PAN FROM THE HEAT AND POUR IN THE CREAM AND SALT. Use a long-handled wooden spoon to carefully stir in the cream, as caramel has a tendency to hiss and splash as the cold cream hits it. Place the pan over low heat and cook, stirring constantly, until the caramel thickens, 5 to 7 minutes. The mixture should be the consistency of very thick cream. Remove from heat and stir in the vanilla and walnuts.

LET THE BOILING SAUCE COOL UNTIL IT IS JUST WARM BEFORE SERVING. To store, cover and refrigerate for up to 1 week. To reheat the sauce, microwave, uncovered, for about 1 minute on high. Stir until smooth. For a mellow, more subdued flavor, allow the caramel to "age" a little (at least overnight) before serving.

If you sip more wine than spirits, the world of whiskey (or whisky if you are in Scotland or Canada) can be a little confusing. The complex flavors of whiskey can bring a wonderful, full-bodied kick to many desserts—especially those with the honeyed flavors of dried fruits, the warmth and crunch of roasted nuts, chewy caramel or butterscotch, and chocolate. If your familiarity with "brown liquor" is minimal, take a peak at this basic overview of whiskey's heavy hitters, to help you pick the one that will best enhance your desserts.

Whiskey is basically a spirit distilled from fermented grains; usually various combinations of corn, barley, wheat, and rye. Although whiskey is made throughout the world, the techniques used to create the spirits from Scotland, Ireland, America, and Canada define its flavor and character.

### SCOTCH WHISKY

Scottish whiskies have a very assertive flavor. Scotch whisky (called "Scotch" in America, but just "whisky" in Britain) is usually divided into three categories: single malt, vatted malt, and blended whisky. Malt Scotch whisky is made with barley that is dried (or "malted") over a peat fire. The smoke from the peat gives this whisky a distinctive earthy, smoky flavor and aroma. Other factors that contribute to whisky's flavor include the distilling process and aging process. Oak casks used previously to age bourbon, sherry, or even port are used to age Scotch whisky, and all contribute their own elusive elements to the final brew. Even the location where the whisky is aged affects the flavor; for example, whisky aged in casks stored near the sea may have an unusual, briny quality. Whisky from Scotland possesses many intense, complex flavors, and can be an acquired taste. Blended varieties may be less asser-tive than the strong, peaty single malts, and are perhaps a good place for a beginner to start experimenting.

### IRISH WHISKEY

Irish whiskey is one of the oldest distilled spirits in Europe, beginning sometime in the mid-twelfth century. Irish whiskey is made from a mixture of grain and barley, similar to blended Scotch, but unlike Scotch, the barley in Irish whiskey is not dried over a peat fire. Therefore it doesn't have the robust smokiness of Scotch. Irish whiskey often uses a combination of malted and "green," or unmalted, barley in its blend, giving the whiskey a fresh, fruity perfume, and a lightly sweet, spicy flavor. Irish whiskey is triple-distilled for an extra-smooth, yet potent finish.

### BOURBON WHISKEY

In 1964 U.S. Congress declared bourbon to be "America's Native Spirit." Created in Kentucky's Bourbon County in the late 1700s, bourbon is a full-bodied corn-based spirit—and must be made with no less than 51 percent and no more than 80 percent corn. It is usually mixed with either rye or wheat (but never both together) and a little barley malt to aid fer-mentation. Wheat and rye add spice and fruitiness to the whiskey. Bourbons made with rye tend to be fiery and bolder than bourbons made with wheat, which have a sweeter, nuttier quality. Bourbon is a hearty, flavorful spirit, and it packs a wallop. It is distilled once and then aged in new charred oak barrels to mellow its flavor and give it a rich, natural caramel color and aroma.

## WHICH WHISKEY?

53

### TENNESSEE WHISKEY

Tennessee whiskey, of which Jack Daniel's is the most famous, is a bourbon whiskey made from corn, rye, and barley, and taken one step further by filtering it through a ten-foot-thick layer of hard sugar-maple charcoal. This filtering process creates a whiskey with a smooth, rich, and spicy flavor and a dark amber color. Tennessee whiskey is made with a "sour mash" process—much like a sourdough starter—where some amount of the fermented mash from a previous batch of whiskey is used in a subsequent batch. This method controls the quality and flavor of the whiskey.

### CANADIAN WHISKY

Canadian whisky, often called rye whisky, is generally lighter and milder than American whiskey. Like Scotch, Canadian whisky is aged in oak barrels previously used to age bourbon or brandy, or sometimes in sherry casks for extra flavor.

# The PUDDING CLUB

Pudding is a soothing thing.
It doesn't require you to be adventurous
or worldly or chic. It isn't intellectually
taxing. Usually one doesn't need to acquire a taste
for pudding, as its soft, enveloping sweetness has a cozy
charm to please every palate.

Every culture has a least a few lush, gooey, spoonable sweets—flan, coeur à la crème, rice and bread puddings—all turning everyday staples into something special. The British hold pudding in such high esteem that they call all desserts "pudding," as if to say, "Here is our standard by which all sweets are judged." Pudding is the ultimate comfort food. When presented with one of the puddings in this chapter, watch your friends and family sigh and smile, nodding their head, shoulders relaxing as they remember the first time they tasted rice pudding, or chocolate custard, or a thick wedge of warm bread pudding drizzled with real caramel. There won't be any tentative looks or nervous comments like, "My, that looks so interesting." Simply the satisfied murmurings of happy taste buds and tummies well filled.

When I am entertaining, I love to make the dessert a day ahead—effortlessly serving something lovely and sweet to my guests at the end of a meal always makes me feel carefree and organized (neither of which I often am). These little cream pots are one of my favorites. The classic butterscotch trinity—butter, brown sugar, and salt—is stirred into a cream base, baked in small coffee cups, and then chilled overnight. I always think of butterscotch as caramel's little sister—a little more laid back, not so complicated, but just as sweet. If you like, before serving these little cream pots, top each one with a tablespoon of soft Butterscotch Sauce.

# Butterscotch Pots SERVES 8

6 TABLESPOONS UNSALTED BUTTER

1½ CUPS FIRMLY PACKED DARK MUSCOVADO SUGAR OR DARK BROWN SUGAR

3½ CUPS HEAVY CREAM

3/4 TEASPOON SALT

1 TABLESPOON PURE VANILLA EXTRACT

1 TABLESPOON SCOTCH WHISKY OR IRISH WHISKEY (SEE PAGE 53)

9 LARGE EGG YOLKS

BOILING WATER AS NEEDED

BUTTERSCOTCH SAUCE (PAGE 139) OR SWEETENED WHIPPED CREAM (PAGE 43) FOR SERVING (OPTIONAL)

POSITION A RACK IN THE MIDDLE OF THE OVEN AND PREHEAT TO 325°F.

IN A LARGE, heavy-bottomed saucepan, combine the butter and brown sugar and melt together over medium heat and bring to a boil. Boil for 1 minute, and then stir in ½ cup of the cream. Stir until the mixture is smooth and combined. Remove from the heat and stir in the remaining 3 cups cream, the salt, vanilla, and whiskey.

IN A LARGE BOWL, whisk the egg yolks until smooth. Gradually whisk the cream mixture into the yolks until smooth. Strain the custard through a fine-mesh sieve into a large container with a pouring spout. Divide the custard among 8 custard cups, ramekins, or ovenproof coffee cups.

PLACE THE CUSTARD CUPS IN A LARGE ROASTING PAN. Place the roasting pan in the oven. Pour boiling water into the roasting pan until it reaches halfway up the sides of the custard cups. Cover the roasting pan with aluminum foil, and pierce it in several places to allow steam to escape.

BAKE THE CUSTARDS JUST UNTIL SET AROUND THE EDGES AND SLIGHTLY WOBBLY IN THE CENTER, 45 minutes to 60 minutes. Remove the custards from the oven and then from the water bath and let cool completely. Cover the custards with plastic wrap and refrigerate until well chilled, at least 4 hours or up to overnight. Top the custards with a tablespoon of Butterscotch Sauce (page 139) or a dollop of whipped cream, if you like, and serve.

"Butter is life."
—INDIAN PROVERB

## CARAMEL AND BUTTERSCOTCH:
*What's the Difference?*

You may think them interchangeable, but caramel and butterscotch, although similar, have very distinctive flavors. Picture the two gals from that television classic *Gilligan's Island*. Think of caramel as the movie star Ginger: smoky and seductive, sophisticated and a little high-maintenance, with just a hint of bittersweetness. Butterscotch is farm girl Mary Ann: easy, sunny and bright, buttery and very sweet, but with a salty edge and a down-to-earth tang.

Caramel is created by slowly heating granulated white sugar until it melts, thickens, and turns the roasted reddish brown color of an old penny. Cooked just to the tipping point of being burnt, caramel has a distinctive, smoky, slightly bitter sweetness that, for desserts and confections, is usually tempered and enriched by the addition of heavy cream.

Butterscotch is made from a combination of dark brown sugar, butter, often a little lemon juice, and a generous dash of salt. The molasses in the brown sugar and the acid in the lemon juice enhance the rich flavor and distinctive sharpness of butterscotch which is mellowed by a generous dollop of butter and that dash of salt. It is this sweet-and-salty savor that gives butterscotch its wonderful flavor. Depending on whether the butterscotch will become a sauce, candy, pudding, or cookies, other ingredients such as corn syrup, milk, or cream may also be added.

Food historians have many theories about the origin of butterscotch. Whether or not its name has anything to do with the country of Scotland is still debated. It may be that once upon a time, buttery toffee was poured and cut, or "scotched," a term from Middle English; or the word "scotch" may be derived from the word "scorched." Either way, the birthplace of butterscotch does seem to be somewhere in the British Isles, but whether in England or Scotland is still unknown.

No recipe collection celebrating all things sticky and gooey would be complete without a recipe for deep, dark, homemade chocolate pudding. It's great alone, or you can make a simple, but delicious, chocolate-caramel trifle by drizzling cubes of Chocolate Pound Cake (page 105) or Devil's Food Cake (page 111) with warm caramel sauce and then top with this rich pudding while it is still warm. Refrigerate the trifle overnight for the flavors to ripen and then cover with a thick blanket of whipped crème fraîche or sweetened whipped cream before serving. Yum!

# Deep, Dark Chocolate Pudding SERVES 4 TO 6

**FOR THE PUDDING:**

6 LARGE EGG YOLKS

2 CUPS HEAVY CREAM

1/4 CUP DUTCH-PROCESSED COCOA POWDER (SEE PAGE 45)

3/4 CUP GRANULATED SUGAR

3 TABLESPOONS CORNSTARCH

1/4 TEASPOON SALT

1½ CUPS WHOLE MILK

8 OUNCES SEMISWEET CHOCOLATE, FINELY CHOPPED

1 TEASPOON PURE VANILLA EXTRACT

**FOR THE WHIPPED CRÈME FRAÎCHE:**

1/2 CUP CRÈME FRAÎCHE

1 CUP HEAVY CREAM

1/4 CUP CONFECTIONERS' SUGAR

1 TEASPOON PURE VANILLA EXTRACT

TO MAKE THE PUDDING: In a large bowl, whisk together the egg yolks and heavy cream. Set aside.

IN A LARGE, heavy-bottomed saucepan, whisk together the cocoa powder, sugar, cornstarch, and salt. Gradually whisk in the milk until smooth. Place over medium heat and cook, stirring constantly with a wooden spoon, just until the mixture begins to boil. Remove from the heat and slowly whisk the hot cocoa mixture into the egg yolks and cream. Pour the egg and cocoa mixture back into the saucepan and continue cooking over medium heat, stirring constantly, just until the mixture begins to boil. Reduce heat to a simmer and continue cooking the pudding for 1 minute, stirring constantly.

REMOVE THE PAN FROM THE HEAT AND POUR THE PUDDING THROUGH A FINE-MESH SIEVE INTO A LARGE BOWL. Stir in the chopped chocolate and vanilla just until the chocolate is melted and the pudding is smooth. Cover the surface of the pudding with plastic wrap to prevent a skin from forming and refrigerate until very cold, at least 3 hours or up to overnight.

RIGHT BEFORE SERVING, MAKE THE WHIPPED CRÈME FRAÎCHE: Combine the crème fraîche, heavy cream, confectioners' sugar, and vanilla in a large metal bowl that has been chilled for 15 minutes in the freezer. Beat with an electric mixer set on medium speed until the creams combine and form soft peaks. Divide the pudding among individual bowls and top with large dollops of the whipped crème fraîche.

When I lived in London, this deliciously sweet, moist, date-speckled cake, covered in a thick, warm layer of butterscotch-toffee sauce, was a fixture on almost every English "pudding" menu. Either invented or simply made famous by Francis Coulson, the owner of the Sharrow Bay Hotel in the Lake District in England, Sticky Toffee Pudding is an addictively simple sweet that is easy to make and easy to love. To prepare this dessert ahead of time, let the cakes cool completely (do not drizzle with sauce). Store in a self-sealing plastic bag in the refrigerator for up to 24 hours. When ready to serve, drizzle each with 1 tablespoon of the toffee sauce and heat in a 350°F oven for 5 minutes or until warmed through.

# Sticky Toffee Pudding SERVES 12 DAINTY, OR 6 RAVENOUS, EATERS

**FOR THE CAKE:**

2 CUPS PITTED DATES (ABOUT 12 OUNCES), PREFERABLY MEDJOOL, CHOPPED

1 1/2 CUPS WATER

1 1/4 TEASPOONS BAKING SODA

2 CUPS BLEACHED ALL-PURPOSE FLOUR

1/2 TEASPOON SALT

1 TEASPOON BAKING POWDER

3/4 CUP (1 1/2 STICKS) UNSALTED BUTTER, AT ROOM TEMPERATURE

1 1/2 CUPS FIRMLY PACKED LIGHT BROWN SUGAR

3 LARGE EGGS

1 TEASPOON PURE VANILLA EXTRACT

**FOR THE TOFFEE SAUCE:**

1 CUP (2 STICKS) UNSALTED BUTTER

3 CUPS FIRMLY PACKED DARK MUSCO-VADO SUGAR OR DARK BROWN SUGAR

2 CUPS HEAVY CREAM

1 TEASPOON PURE VANILLA EXTRACT

1/4 TEASPOON SALT

VANILLA ICE CREAM FOR SERVING

LIGHTLY BUTTER A STANDARD 12-CUP MUFFIN TIN OR SPRAY WITH NONSTICK COOKING SPRAY. Position a rack in the middle of the oven and preheat to 350°F.

TO MAKE THE CAKE: Combine the dates and water in a heavy-bottomed saucepan. Bring to a gentle boil. Reduce the heat to a simmer, and cook, uncovered, until the dates are softened and have absorbed the water. Remove from the heat and stir in 1 teaspoon of the baking soda. Let stand for about 20 minutes.

WHILE THE DATES ARE SOAKING, sift together the flour, salt, remaining 1/4 teaspoon baking soda, and the baking powder into a bowl. Set aside. In another bowl, beat together the butter and brown sugar until light and fluffy. Beat in the eggs, one at a time, beating well after each addition, and then beat in the vanilla. Stir the dates and any soaking liquid into the batter. Gently fold the dry ingredients into the wet batter just until combined.

FILL THE MUFFIN CUPS TWO-THIRDS FULL. Bake until a wooden skewer inserted in the center of a cake comes out clean, 22 to 28 minutes.

MEANWHILE, MAKE THE TOFFEE SAUCE: Combine the butter and brown sugar in a saucepan over medium heat. Cook until the sugar and butter melt together. Add the cream, vanilla, and salt. Increase the heat to high and bring to a boil. Reduce the heat to a simmer and cook, stirring frequently, until the sauce thickens, 6 to 8 minutes.

REMOVE THE CAKES FROM THE OVEN AND POKE THE TOP OF EACH A FEW TIMES WITH A WOODEN SKEWER. Drizzle 1 tablespoon of the warm sauce over each cake and allow it to sink in completely.

TO SERVE, spoon a little sauce on each dessert plate and place a cake, top-side down, in the sauce. Spoon more warm sauce over the top of the cake and serve immediately, with a big scoop of vanilla ice cream.

## THE CHARM OF BRITISH PUDDING

With the ink freshly dried on both my marriage certificate and my diploma from Le Cordon Bleu Cooking School, I landed my first job working as a director's chef in a large advertising agency in London. It was a great job. No nights. No weekends. No budget. When I say no budget, I mean no budget constraints; there were endless funds to rustle up all the fancy food my newly minted cooking skills could conjure. I was ecstatic. I made lots of plans, lists, and menus. My only limitation was Pixie. Pixie hired me. Pixie had seniority. Pixie was a skinflint. Pixie was a thin-lipped, thin-hipped, redheaded Scottish woman, and a careful and simple cook. She hated garlic, she hated fancy desserts, and after a while I was not so sure she was very fond of me. Pixie loved smoked salmon, which we served incessantly, and she had a notorious predilection for pilfering the leftovers. Fresh with the snobbery of youth and a cooking school diploma, I wanted to wrap giant prawns in prosciutto for grilling, and make endlessly fiddly little lemon soufflés with citrus suprêmes; she wanted grilled trout and boiled potatoes. We had a standoff. When I wanted to fill squeeze bottles with raspberry coulis and decorate the dessert plates with little hearts and spiderwebs (the squeeze bottle was my favorite '80s kitchen tool—I never went anywhere without at least one), she just rolled her eyes. Good, solid British food had been good enough before I arrived and it would still be good enough after I left.

In December, as the weather grew bitter, Pixie informed me that we would be preparing a full Christmas dinner, every day, for various in-house office parties the entire month. But there would be no bûche de Noël, or decorated Christmas cookies, but instead twenty days of Pixie's version of a traditional British turkey dinner. I was unfamiliar with many of the traditional accoutrements, but after the first week, we hit our stride and had the preparation down to a science. Pixie unwrapped little chipolata sausages delivered from the butcher every morning and fried them to go along with the roasted bird. She loaded her stuffing with dried apricots and cooked it in a casserole dish. I peeled endless potatoes to roast (not mash) and Pixie taught me how to make bread sauce—a soft gruel of fresh white bread crumbs cooked in an onion-and-clove-scented milky broth, liberally laced with lots of butter.

Sounds horrifying, doesn't it? I thought so, too. But it is delicious. I had never made bread sauce before and I never have since, but I loved it. Pixie was delighted. After that, I made the hard sauce for, of course, our Christmas puddings. Hard sauce is just butter and confectioners' sugar beaten together and doused with as much lung-searing brandy as it will hold without liquefying. Pixie purchased her puddings from Fortnum and Mason, the historic London specialty-goods store. Twenty puddings arrived in their own porcelain basins wrapped in muslin pudding cloth for steaming. I had no idea what to expect from a real English Christmas pudding, but I read Dickens. I was game. When Pixie slid the solid, steaming, black pudding onto a silver tray, I was so disappointed. How could we possibly gussy up this lump and make it festive? But she ladled on the brandy and topped it with a jaunty sprig of holly, and we turned off the lights in the dining room when we lit the pudding afire. Every day, after each turkey, every party erupted in cheers when that blazing lump was strutted in. I was sure it had more to do with scarfing down the brandy-soaked hard sauce than anything else. There was always a little pudding left over at the end of each meal and Pixie always wanted me to try it, but I still clung to the vision of that bûche de Noël dancing in my head and either out of stubbornness or fatigue, I always declined. Until the twentieth Christmas dinner. Our last turkey. Our last "pud." So I scooped a little of that dark mass onto a plate, allowed myself a hefty dollop of hard sauce, and dug in. Never, ever, judge a book by its cover. The pudding wasn't heavy, but moist and delicate, with an unctuous, spicy, brandy-soaked flavor, rich with dried fruits, with no one element dominating, but rather all of them melding into one, mysterious, festive, and completely distinct and recognizable taste I can only describe as "Christmas." After that, Pixie and I came to an understanding. I never mentioned the smoked salmon and she let me keep my squeeze bottles and make frozen mud pie and pretend I invented it.

Since then, I have always had a soft spot in my heart for British puddings. Sweet steamed and baked puddings are so numerous in British cookery that "pudding" has become synonymous with any dessert served at the end of a meal. It's hard not to smile at the thought of Sticky Toffee Pudding (page 61),

or wonder if Prince Charles enjoys a little bit of Eton Mess (page 74) every now and again. No one can really resist a trifle, which is just another way of ingesting as much English double cream as possible. Rhubarb and apple crumbles, served with "lashings of custard" or clotted cream, syllabubs, fools, fairy cakes, and summer pudding all have their distinct and comforting charms. English bakeries are stuffed with treats like lardy cakes, Bakewell Tart, and Victoria Sandwich—the latter just simple, moist sponge cake layered with a sticky jam and whipped cream filling. As much as I love the chic elegance of *île flottante* and *coeur à la crème*, they don't have the same Tom-Kitten lovability of Jam Roly-Poly and Marmalade Sponge.

The Pudding Club, an English organization founded in 1985, began specifically to promote baking and eating more classic British puddings, and to battle back against the invasion of foreign upstarts like tiramisu and chocolate cheesecake. The Three Ways House Hotel in Mickleton, Gloucestershire, is home to the Pudding Club, and members meet often to indulge in sometimes up to seven different types of pudding in one sitting (the only caveat: you must clean your plate before you sample another flavor). So here's to the Pudding Club, celebrating the slightly matronly, stodgy glamour of the "squidgy" British "pud." Long may it reign.

*"Nearly eleven o'clock," Pooh said happily.*
*"You're just in time for a little smackeral of something..."*
—FROM *THE HOUSE AT POOH CORNER*, BY A. A. MILNE

63

I adapted this recipe for old-fashioned Christmas pudding from my copy of the *Harrods Cookery Book*. It's a traditional recipe for a classic English Christmas treat. Whatever you do, don't skimp on the hard sauce. Make sure to make this pudding at least 1 week before you want to serve it.

# Christmas Pudding with Brandied Hard Sauce

SERVES 8 TO 10

1 1/3 CUPS DRIED CURRANTS

1 1/3 CUPS RAISINS

1 1/3 CUPS GOLDEN RAISINS

1 CUP DRIED FIGS, VERY FINELY CHOPPED

3/4 CUP BRANDY

1 LARGE GRANNY SMITH APPLE, PEELED, CORED, AND FINELY GRATED

GRATED ZEST AND JUICE OF 1 ORANGE

GRATED ZEST AND JUICE OF 1 LEMON

1/2 CUP SHREDDED BEEF SUET, OR 3/4 CUP (1 1/2 STICKS) UNSALTED BUTTER OR 3/4 CUP COCONUT OIL, MELTED (SEE RECIPE INTRODUCTION PAGE 126)

2 CUPS SHREDDED FRESH WHITE BREAD CRUMBS

1 1/4 CUPS FINELY GROUND ALMONDS (SEE PAGE 89)

1 1/4 CUPS ALL-PURPOSE FLOUR

1 TEASPOON BAKING POWDER

1/4 TEASPOON BAKING SODA

1 1/2 TEASPOONS GROUND CINNAMON

1 TEASPOON GROUND GINGER

1/2 TEASPOON CLOVES

1/2 TEASPOON GROUND NUTMEG

GREASE A 2 1/4-QUART HEATPROOF PUDDING BASIN OR CERAMIC BOWL WITH SOFTENED BUTTER. Set aside.

IN A LARGE SAUCEPAN, combine the currants, raisins, golden raisins, dried figs, and brandy over medium-low heat. Cover and simmer for 5 minutes. Remove from heat and let cool completely. When cool, stir in the grated apple and orange and lemon zests and juices.

IN A LARGE BOWL, toss together the beef suet (if using instead of the butter or coconut oil), bread crumbs, ground almonds, flour, baking powder, baking soda, cinnamon, ginger, cloves, nutmeg, and salt.

IN ANOTHER BOWL, beat together the butter or coconut oil (if using instead of the beef suet), eggs, sugar, and vanilla until creamy. Use a rubber spatula to stir the dried fruit and brandy mixture into the egg mixture. Carefully fold in the bread-crumb mixture until combined.

POUR THE BATTER INTO THE PREPARED PUDDING BASIN AND COVER THE BATTER WITH A CIRCLE OF BUTTERED PARCHMENT PAPER THAT FITS INSIDE THE RIM OF THE BASIN. Cover the basin with a double layer of aluminum foil, crimping it well around the rim.

PLACE A HEATPROOF TRIVET IN THE BOTTOM OF A DUTCH OVEN OR STOCK POT. Lower the pudding into the saucepan onto the trivet and fill with enough boiling water to come two-thirds of the way up the sides of the basin. Place the Dutch oven over medium-low heat, cover, and simmer the pudding gently until it is firm, 6 hours. Check the water level occasionally, refilling with more boiling water as needed.

I spent one semester in London during my junior year in college and I still remember my first visit to Harrods, known for carrying the most rare and elusive items. It used to be said that you could buy anything at Harrods, from a pin to an elephant, and the lavish displays in their famous Food Halls do little to dispel that hyperbole. I still remember rabbits hanging above the game counter, fur intact, and fat turkeys, plucked, but with heads still dangling, ready to be wrapped up and sent on their way. The fruit and vegetable section, or "hall," is a fragrant, colorful still life lovingly displayed and devoted to every type of produce imaginable, at their peak of ripeness. Of course, there is a charcuterie, a dairy with hundreds of different cheeses resting on marble slabs, a bakery, and an ice cream parlor, and on my last visit, I noticed a miniature Krispy Kreme donut shop tucked in next to the confectionery hall. Rare and elusive, indeed.

1/2 TEASPOON SALT

3 LARGE EGGS

1 CUP FIRMLY PACKED DARK MUSCOVADO OR DARK BROWN SUGAR

2 TEASPOONS PURE VANILLA EXTRACT

SPRIG OF HOLLY

1/2 CUP BRANDY

1 TEASPOON SUGAR

BRANDIED HARD SAUCE (RECIPE FOLLOWS)

WHEN THE PUDDING IS DONE, remove the pan from the heat and let cool slightly. When cool enough to touch, lift the pudding basin out of the water and transfer to a wire rack to finish cooling. Remove the foil and circle of parchment paper from the pudding and cover the cooled pudding with plastic wrap. Refrigerate the pudding until ready to serve.

TO SERVE, cover the pudding with buttered foil and crimp around the edge of the basin and steam as before until very hot, 2 to 3 hours. Remove the foil and invert the pudding onto a serving platter. Garnish the top with the sprig of holly. Heat the brandy and sugar in a small saucepan until warm. Pour over the pudding and flame with a long wooden match or grill lighter. Serve the pudding while aflame, with the Brandied Hard Sauce.

## Brandied Hard Sauce MAKES 1 CUP

2 STICKS UNSALTED BUTTER, AT ROOM TEMPERATURE

3 TO 4 CUPS CONFECTIONERS' SUGAR, SIFTED

GRATED ZEST OF 1 LEMON

1/2 CUP BRANDY

IN A BOWL USING AN ELECTRIC MIXER SET AT MEDIUM SPEED, cream the butter and 3 cups of the confectioners' sugar until light and creamy. Beat in the lemon zest. Gradually beat in the brandy, a little at a time, until well blended. Taste the hard sauce, and if you want it sweeter, beat in the remaining sugar. Store in a covered container for up to 2 weeks before serving. Let the hard sauce soften a little at room temperature before serving with the pudding.

My husband, Jim, tasted banana bread pudding at one of his favorite San Francisco restaurants and raved about it for months. He asked me to duplicate it and finally I relented. When he said "banana bread pudding," I thought he meant a bread pudding made with banana bread. Not exactly what he had in mind. His response was less than enthusiastic, and I realized you can't have a thin skin when testing new recipes. My second attempt, however, hit the mark: a cream-rich, eggy custard spiked with ripe bananas and combined with fat cubes of cinnamon-toasted, buttery brioche. Heaven for banana—and comfort food—lovers alike. It only gets better when drizzled with warm, dark chocolate sauce and a generous sprinkling of toasted walnuts.

# Banana Bread Pudding
## with Hot Fudge and Toasted Walnuts SERVES 8 TO 10

1 LOAF BRIOCHE (13 OUNCES), CUT CROSSWISE INTO 12 SLICES ABOUT 1 INCH THICK

3/4 CUP (1 1/2 STICKS) UNSALTED BUTTER, MELTED, PLUS 2 TABLESPOONS COLD BUTTER, CUT INTO LITTLE BITS

1 1/2 CUPS SUGAR

1 TABLESPOON GROUND CINNAMON

8 LARGE EGGS

3 LARGE EGG YOLKS

1 TEASPOON PURE VANILLA EXTRACT

2 CUPS HEAVY CREAM

1 CUP WHOLE MILK

1/8 TEASPOON SALT

1 CUP MASHED RIPE BANANAS

MY FAVORITE GANACHE (PAGE 29)

1 CUP COARSELY CHOPPED WALNUTS, TOASTED (SEE PAGE 89)

VANILLA ICE CREAM OR SWEETENED WHIPPED CREAM (PAGE 43) FOR SERVING (OPTIONAL)

POSITION A RACK IN THE MIDDLE OF THE OVEN AND PREHEAT TO 350°F. Lightly butter a 9-by-13-inch rectangular or oval baking dish.

BRUSH BOTH SIDES OF THE BRIOCHE SLICES WITH THE MELTED BUTTER. Stir together 1/2 cup of the sugar with the cinnamon. Sprinkle both sides of the buttered brioche with the cinnamon-sugar, reserving 2 tablespoons for topping the pudding. Cut each slice into 4 squares (like big croutons), place on a baking sheet, and toast in the oven until golden brown and crisp all over, tossing occasionally, 7 to 10 minutes. Let cool completely.

IN A LARGE BOWL BIG ENOUGH TO HOLD THE CUSTARD AND THE BREAD, whisk together the whole eggs, egg yolks, the remaining 1 cup sugar, and the vanilla. Gradually whisk in the cream and milk. Stir in the salt and mashed bananas. Add the brioche croutons and stir to coat them with the custard.

POUR THE PUDDING MIXTURE INTO THE PREPARED DISH. Cover the dish with plastic wrap and refrigerate for at least 4 hours or up to overnight to allow the bread to absorb much of the custard.

PREHEAT THE OVEN TO 325°F. Remove the pudding from the refrigerator and dot the top with the cold butter bits. Sprinkle with the reserved 2 tablespoons cinnamon-sugar. Cover the bread pudding with aluminum foil. Pierce a few holes in the foil to allow steam to escape. Bake for 20 minutes. Uncover the pudding and continue baking until it is puffed and golden and when a knife inserted into the center of the pudding comes out clean, 20 to 25 minutes. Let cool for 5 minutes. Cut the pudding into squares and drizzle each serving with ganache and a sprinkling of walnuts. Serve warm, with vanilla ice cream or whipped cream, if desired.

We lived in Hawaii for a year when my oldest daughter, Olivia, was four years old. I read her a story about volcanoes before we moved, to get her excited about what she would see when we arrived on the Big Island. She called the lava "glava," and the name has stuck in our family ever since. That's what the thick, chocolate-caramel sauce spooned over this rich pudding reminds me of—a slow-moving, burnished, molten ooze, slipping into the crevices of the pudding with the same impossible-to-resist tenacity of the real thing. This pudding is fine served warm or cold, but the sauce should be warm, for the proper oozing effect.

# Chocolate Croissant Bread Pudding with Hot "Glava" Sauce SERVES 10 TO 12

6 DAY-OLD CROISSANTS

8 LARGE EGGS

2 CUPS SUGAR, PLUS 2 TO 3 TABLE-SPOONS FOR SPRINKLING

4 CUPS HEAVY CREAM

1/4 TEASPOON SALT

2 TEASPOONS PURE VANILLA EXTRACT

1/4 CUP KAHLÚA, DARK RUM, OR IRISH WHISKEY

8 OUNCES SEMI-SWEET OR BITTER-SWEET CHOCOLATE, FINELY CHOPPED

SPLIT THE CROISSANTS IN HALF LENGTHWISE. Lightly butter a 9-by-13-inch baking dish or 3-quart soufflé dish. Place the bottom halves of the croissants into the dish, cut-side up, squeezing them in to fit. Set aside the croissant tops.

IN A LARGE BOWL, whisk together the eggs and the 2 cups sugar until smooth. Slowly whisk in 3 cups of the heavy cream. Stir in the salt, vanilla, and Kahlúa.

IN A HEAVY-BOTTOMED SAUCEPAN OVER MEDIUM HEAT, heat the remaining 1 cup of cream just until it starts to boil. Remove the pan from the heat and stir in the chocolate until the chocolate is melted and the mixture is smooth and creamy. Let cool slightly. Whisk the chocolate cream into the egg custard until dark and smooth.

POUR HALF OF THE CUSTARD THROUGH A FINE-MESH SIEVE OVER THE CROISSANTS IN THE BAKING DISH, making sure the croissants are coated with the chocolate custard. Arrange the croissant tops over the custard, squeezing them tightly into the pan if necessary. Strain the remaining custard over the croissants to thoroughly coat them. Cover the dish with plastic wrap and place a smaller dish over the plastic wrap. This will help keep the croissants submerged in the custard. Let the pudding stand for at least 1 hour to allow the croissants to get soaked through. (The pudding can also be prepared in the morning and refrigerated all day until the evening and baked right before serving.)

*"The smell of chocolate bubbling over and slightly burning is one of the most beautiful smells in the world. It is subtle and comforting and it is rich. One tiny drop perfumes a room as nothing else."*
—FROM HOME COOKING, BY LAURIE COLWIN

**FOR THE HOT "GLAVA" SAUCE:**

1 CUP SUGAR

1/4 CUP WATER

2 CUPS HEAVY CREAM

PINCH OF SALT

1 TEASPOON PURE VANILLA EXTRACT

2 TABLESPOONS KAHLÚA, DARK RUM, OR IRISH WHISKEY

8 OUNCES SEMISWEET CHOCOLATE, FINELY CHOPPED, OR 1 HEAPING CUP SEMISWEET CHOCOLATE CHIPS

SWEETENED WHIPPED CREAM (PAGE 43) OR VANILLA ICE CREAM FOR SERVING (OPTIONAL)

POSITION RACK IN THE MIDDLE OF THE OVEN AND PREHEAT TO 325°F. Remove the plate and plastic wrap from the pudding and sprinkle it with the 2 to 3 tablespoons sugar. Bake until a knife inserted into the center of the pudding comes out clean, 45 to 60 minutes.

MEANWHILE, MAKE THE "GLAVA" SAUCE: Combine the sugar and the water in a large, heavy-bottomed saucepan over medium heat. Cook, gently swirling the pan occasionally, until the syrup dissolves and starts to turn color. Bring to a boil and cook until the syrup turns a deep amber color, 4 to 5 minutes. Watch carefully as it can burn easily and quickly.

IMMEDIATELY REMOVE THE PAN FROM THE HEAT AND STIR IN THE CREAM AND SALT. Use a long-handled wooden spoon to carefully stir the mixture, as the caramel has a tendency to hiss and splash as the cream hits it. Place the pan over low heat and cook, stirring constantly, until the caramel thickens, 4 to 5 minutes. Remove the sauce from the heat and stir in the vanilla and Kahlúa. Stir the chocolate into the warm sauce until it is completely melted and combined.

REMOVE THE PUDDING FROM THE OVEN AND COOL SLIGHTLY. Cut the warm pudding into 10 to 12 portions. Top each portion with a ladle full of warm chocolate "glava" sauce and serve with the whipped cream or ice cream, if desired.

"Toothsome" may seem a word more suited to a pirate's description of a voluptuous and saucy wench, but it also means delicious, sumptuous, mouthwatering. There is also a certain sense of easy comfort (in both the wench and the food) that it describes. This risotto rice pudding is just such a dish; voluptuously creamy, with firm but tender grains of Arborio rice suspended in a creamy yolk-tinged, vanilla-scented, milky pudding. It's always amazing to me how little rice you really need to make a good rice pudding—remember, it's the milk that makes the dish, reducing as the rice cooks. This robust rice pudding firms up remarkably as it cools, so don't be nervous about all that milk as you first begin to cook it!

# Rich Risotto Rice Pudding  SERVES 4 TO 6

1/2 CUP ARBORIO RICE

8 CUPS WHOLE MILK

1/2 CUP SUGAR

1 VANILLA BEAN, SPLIT IN HALF LENGTHWISE

1/4 TEASPOON GROUND CINNAMON

1/4 TEASPOON SALT

2 LARGE EGG YOLKS

1/2 CUP HEAVY CREAM

2 TEASPOONS PURE VANILLA EXTRACT

FRESHLY GRATED NUTMEG (OPTIONAL)

COMBINE THE RICE, milk, sugar, vanilla bean, cinnamon, and salt in a large heavy-bottomed saucepan over medium-high heat and stir to combine. Bring the mixture to a boil, stirring constantly. Reduce the heat to medium-low and simmer, stirring every 5 minutes as the mixture starts to thicken, for about 30 minutes. Continue cooking until the rice is tender but not too mushy, about 15 minutes longer. The milk will be thick and the rice tender, but the mixture will still be a little soupy, which is what you want. (As the pudding cools, it thickens, and if it is too thick while still hot, it will firm up into a thick, stodgy lump without the unctuous creaminess of a great rice pudding.)

IN A BOWL, whisk the egg yolks and cream together and stir into the rice pudding. Continue cooking the pudding over medium-low heat for 2 to 3 minutes, until the eggs are cooked through and pudding is creamy and glossy, but still fairly soupy. Remove from the heat and stir in the vanilla. Grate a little nutmeg (if using) into the pudding. Remove the vanilla bean. Pour the pudding into a serving bowl and press plastic wrap over the surface to prevent a skin from forming. Refrigerate until cold, at least 2 to 3 hours. Serve cold.

NOTE: THIS PUDDING IS DELICIOUS AS IT IS, or you can fold a dollop of whipped cream into each serving, or layer the pudding in a parfait glass with dulce de leche or caramel sauce, or just drizzle some sauce on top before serving.

While researching recipes for this book, I came across a few for donut bread pudding, and I have to admit, I was intrigued. Most used simple glazed donuts and a thick custard made with sweetened condensed milk, but I couldn't resist trying my own version using glazed cinnamon-roll donuts from Stardust Donuts, a little ramshackle donut stand at the edge of Imperial Beach, a tiny California beach community near my home. Use your own favorite donut shop cinnamon-swirled yeast-raised donut in your version of this pudding. Bake the puddings in individual coffee cups and serve them warm.

# Cinnamon-Donut Bread Pudding SERVES 6

**FOR THE CINNAMON CUSTARD SAUCE:**

5 LARGE EGG YOLKS

1/2 CUP SUGAR

1 TEASPOON PURE VANILLA EXTRACT

1/2 TEASPOON GROUND CINNAMON

2 CUPS HEAVY CREAM

**FOR THE PUDDING:**

4 LARGE EGGS

4 LARGE EGG YOLKS

1/4 TEASPOON SALT

2 TEASPOONS PURE VANILLA EXTRACT

2 CUPS HEAVY CREAM

1/2 CUP WHOLE MILK

1/2 CUP GRANULATED SUGAR, PLUS 6 TEASPOONS FOR SPRINKLING

1/4 CUP FIRMLY PACKED LIGHT BROWN SUGAR

1 1/2 TEASPOONS GROUND CINNAMON, PLUS EXTRA FOR SPRINKLING

1/4 TEASPOON GROUND GINGER

1 POUND (5 OR 6) DAY-OLD, YEAST-RAISED CINNAMON-ROLL DONUTS, CUT INTO 1-INCH PIECES

BOILING WATER AS NEEDED

VANILLA ICE CREAM FOR SERVING (OPTIONAL)

TO MAKE THE SAUCE: Whisk together the egg yolks, sugar, vanilla, and cinnamon in a bowl until smooth. Heat the cream in a heavy-bottomed saucepan over medium heat just until it comes to a boil. Remove the pan from the heat and whisk the hot cream into the egg yolks, 1/4 cup at a time, until all the cream has been slowly incorporated into the egg yolks.

RETURN THE ENTIRE MIXTURE TO THE SAUCEPAN AND COOK OVER LOW HEAT, stirring constantly, until the custard is thickened and coats the back of a wooden spoon. Do not boil, or the custard will curdle. Immediately pour the custard through a fine-mesh sieve into a bowl and whisk until very smooth, about 1 minute. Let cool to room temperature, then cover the bowl with plastic wrap and refrigerate until very cold, 2 to 3 hours or up to overnight.

TO MAKE THE PUDDING: In a bowl, whisk together the eggs, egg yolks, salt, vanilla, heavy cream, milk, granulated and brown sugars, cinnamon, and ginger until smooth. Place the donut pieces in a large bowl. Pour the custard over the donuts pieces and let stand for 1 hour to allow the donuts to absorb the custard. Divide the mixture evenly and spoon into 6 ovenproof coffee cups that have been brushed with melted butter. Sprinkle each with 1 teaspoon of the remaining granulated sugar and a pinch of cinnamon.

POSITION A RACK IN THE MIDDLE OF THE OVEN AND PREHEAT TO 350°F. Place the cups in a large roasting pan and place the pan in the oven. Fill the pan with boiling water until it reaches halfway up the sides of the cups and cover with aluminum foil. Bake for 30 minutes. Remove the foil and continue baking until pudding is puffed and golden and a knife comes out clean when inserted into the center of a pudding, 15 to 20 minutes longer. Let cool for 10 to 15 minutes.

SERVE THE PUDDINGS WARM, drizzled with the cold cinnamon custard sauce and/or a scoop of vanilla ice cream, if desired.

## GRANULATED SUGAR

Granulated sugar is the refined white sugar extracted from either sugarcane or sugar beets. Although, chemically, sugarcane and sugar beet sugars are the same, many bakers and pastry chefs prefer the flavor and texture of candies and baked goods prepared from cane sugar. The flavor differences may be minor, but beet sugar can sometimes be difficult to caramelize, so for butterscotch, caramel sauces, and other recipes requiring caramelization, use cane sugar.

## SUPERFINE SUGAR

Also known as bar sugar or caster sugar, this white sugar has very fine granules that dissolve easily and blend thoroughly, leaving no trace of grittiness. Superfine sugar works beautifully in finely textured genoise and angel food cakes and in meringues, where it minimizes the chances of undissolved sugars "beading" or "weeping." Superfine sugar is usually available in 1-pound boxes, but if you can't find it, you can make your own reasonable facsimile by buzzing regular granulated sugar for a few seconds in a food processor.

## CONFECTIONERS' SUGAR

Also known as powdered sugar or icing sugar, confectioners' sugar is granulated sugar that has been ground to a powder with cornstarch added to prevent lumping and crystallization. Confectioners' sugar dissolves easily and completely. It is used in uncooked buttercreams, glazes, meringues, some cookies and pastries, and as a decorative accent.

## BROWN SUGAR

Refined granulated sugar is combined and processed with different amounts of molasses added back in to create light and dark brown sugar. Brown sugar has a moist, slightly grainy texture and a light, caramel-like molasses flavor. Desserts made with moist sugars like brown sugar tend to have a moister texture themselves, and stay fresher longer. Due to its moisture content, brown sugar can get lumpy and hard if it is left to dry out in the air. To prevent this, store brown sugar in a tightly sealed container or self-sealing plastic bag. Brown sugar is excellent in moist, sticky gingerbread and spice cake, coffee and chocolate desserts, and is the main ingredient in all butterscotch desserts.

## MUSCOVADO SUGAR

Unlike light and dark brown sugar, muscovado sugar is a raw, unrefined brown cane sugar. It is moist and slightly sticky with a strong, rich, slightly rummy flavor redolent of molasses and spice. It can be used interchangeably with light and dark brown sugar, and is definitely worth seeking out. Muscovado sugar is very popular in England, and is thus sometimes called "British sugar." It is usually available in 8-ounce or 1-pound packets from whole-food and health-food stores, as well as some upscale grocers and kitchenware shops.

## DEMERARA SUGAR

Similar to muscovado, demerara is another caramel-colored raw sugar with a medium grain and a mild hint of molasses. This crystal sugar can be used as a table sugar, and is a frequent choice for rolling gingersnap and other cookie doughs in,

### GIVE ME SOME SUGAR
{ *Facts* }

decorating baked cookies, and sprinkling over the tops of bread pudding and custards. It is available in well-stocked grocery stores, whole-food and health-food stores.

## TURBINADO SUGAR

This raw sugar has larger, paler, crystals than demerara sugar, and a mellow honey flavor. Turbinado sugar melts into a beautifully crisp, glistening amber shell atop crème brûlée. It is available where muscovado and demerara sugars are sold.

This simple fruit-and-cream "pudding" was created at Eton College, the prestigious boys' school founded by King Henry VIII near Windsor, England, famous for educating prime ministers, artists, writers, and royalty—even occasional fictional characters, from *Bridget Jones*'s Mark Darcy to James Bond. Perhaps more interesting is the list of "Non-Etonians," posted by the college's Web site, including those who some may think attended this illustrious academy but, the college is very keen to elucidate, did not. Winston Churchill is on the list and so, oddly enough, is Harland "Colonel" Sanders—yes, the Kentucky Fried One himself. For a time-saving version, feel free to use store-bought meringues.

# Eton Mess SERVES 6 TO 8

**FOR THE MERINGUES:**

4 LARGE EGG WHITES, AT ROOM TEMPERATURE

1/4 TEASPOON CREAM OF TARTAR

PINCH OF SALT

2/3 CUP SUPERFINE SUGAR

1 TEASPOON VANILLA

2/3 CUP CONFECTIONERS' SUGAR, SIFTED

**FOR THE ETON MESS:**

1 POUND FRESH STRAWBERRIES, SLICED

2 CUPS FROZEN STRAWBERRIES, THAWED

1 CUP CONFECTIONERS' SUGAR, SIFTED

2 CUPS HEAVY CREAM

1/2 CUP SOUR CREAM

10 TO 15 TWO-INCH MERINGUE COOKIES, HOMEMADE OR STORE-BOUGHT

PREPARE THE MERINGUES AT LEAST ONE DAY BEFORE SERVING FINAL DESSERT.

TO MAKE THE MERINGUES: Position a rack on the middle shelf of the oven and place a second rack on the top shelf. Preheat the oven to 250°F. Line two baking sheets with parchment paper.

IN A LARGE METAL BOWL, beat the egg whites and cream of tartar with an electric mixer set at low speed until foamy. Add the salt, increase the mixer speed to medium-high, and continue beating until soft peaks form. Add the superfine sugar 1 tablespoon at a time, beating constantly until stiff peaks form. Beat in the vanilla.

SIFT THE CONFECTIONERS' SUGAR A SECOND TIME OVER THE EGG WHITES. Using a rubber spatula, carefully fold the sugar into the egg whites just until no streaks of confectioners' sugar remain. Do not overmix, as this will deflate the meringue.

USING A LARGE SERVING SPOON, scoop 8 to 10 large 1/4-cup portions of the meringue onto each prepared baking sheet.

*"If the English can survive their food, they can survive anything."*
—GEORGE BERNARD SHAW

**PLACE BOTH SHEETS OF MERINGUES IN THE OVEN.** Reduce the oven temperature to 200°F and bake until very crisp, about 2 hours. Baking the meringues for a long period of time at a low temperature assures that they will remain white and become very crisp. If the meringues begin to color, prop the oven door open with the handle of a wooden spoon. When the meringues are done, turn the oven off and let them cool in the oven for at least 1 and up to 6 hours.

**USE IMMEDIATELY,** or store the cooled meringues in a tightly covered container for up to 1 week.

**TO MAKE THE "MESS":** Place the fresh strawberries in a large bowl. Set aside. Process the thawed frozen strawberries in a blender or food processor until they form a thick purée. Stir 1/2 cup of the confectioners' sugar into the purée. Toss the fresh strawberries with sweetened strawberry purée.

**USING AN ELECTRIC MIXER SET AT MEDIUM SPEED,** whip the cream and remaining confectioners' sugar together in a chilled bowl until soft peaks form, about 4 to 5 minutes. Use a rubber spatula to fold in the sour cream.

**BREAK MERINGUE COOKIES INTO LARGE,** bite-size pieces. Fold the meringues and cream into the strawberries just until combined. Do not overmix; the finished dessert should be a billowy, pink-streaked confection, with visible chunks of ruby berries and crunchy chunks of meringue. Spoon the dessert into a large serving bowl and serve immediately.

When it comes to coconut, I find people either love it or loathe it. There really is no waffling when it comes to this, in my mind, luscious nut. I adore coconut, and I have a soft spot for any recipe that features it. Although I usually find flan a little bouncy and gelatinous, this version is dense and succulent, made velvety with the addition of cream cheese and rich with the sweetness of coconut.

# Coconut Milk–Cream Cheese Flan

SERVES 6 TO 8

**FOR THE CARAMEL:**

1 CUP SUGAR

2 TABLESPOONS WATER

1/2 TEASPOON FRESH LEMON JUICE

**FOR THE CUSTARD:**

TWO 8-OUNCE PACKAGES CREAM CHEESE

1 CUP CANNED COCONUT MILK (SEE PAGE 78)

1/2 CUP CREAM OF COCONUT (SEE PAGE 78)

1 CAN (14 OUNCES) SWEETENED CONDENSED MILK

7 LARGE EGGS

1/2 TEASPOON PURE VANILLA EXTRACT

1/4 TEASPOON SALT

BOILING WATER AS NEEDED

**TO MAKE THE CARAMEL:** Combine the sugar, water, and lemon juice in a large, heavy-bottomed saucepan over medium heat. Cook, gently swirling the pan occasionally, until the sugar dissolves and starts to turn color. Increase the heat to high and boil until the syrup turns a deep amber color, 4 to 5 minutes. If the mixture gets too brown it will start to smoke and smell burned and the caramel will be ruined, forcing you to discard this mess and start again. Once you begin making the caramel, do not leave the pot! Caramel can go from perfection to disaster in just seconds.

**IMMEDIATELY POUR THE CARAMEL INTO A 9-INCH CAKE PAN,** swirl to completely coat the bottom and halfway up the sides of the pan, and set aside.

**TO MAKE THE CUSTARD:** In a blender or food processor, combine all the custard ingredients (except the boiling water) and blend or pulse on low speed just until smooth and combined. Strain the custard through a fine-mesh sieve into the caramel-lined pan.

**POSITION A RACK IN THE MIDDLE OF THE OVEN AND PREHEAT TO 300°F.** Place the cake pan in a larger roasting pan and place the roasting pan on the oven rack. Pour boiling water into the roasting pan until it reaches halfway up the sides of the cake pan. Cover the roasting pan with aluminum foil, piercing the foil in several places to allow steam to escape. Bake until the flan is firm to the touch in the center and doesn't jiggle when the pan is moved, 50 to 60 minutes.

**TRANSFER THE FLAN FROM THE WATER BATH TO A WIRE RACK AND LET COOL.** When completely cool, cover with plastic wrap and refrigerate until very cold, preferably overnight.

**TO UNMOLD,** run a table knife carefully around the edges of the pan, pressing it against the side of the pan to loosen the flan but avoiding cutting into the custard. Hold a serving platter (one large enough to hold the lovely, golden sauce) over the top of the flan and invert. Shake the pan gently to release the custard. Remove the pan and let the caramel sauce flow around the sides of the flan and pool around the edges of the serving plate. Serve immediately.

The nutty, tropical flavor of coconut is the perfect addition to many sticky chewy cookies, cream pies, and cakes. Coconut is available in many forms:

### COCONUT MILK

Coconut milk is a creamy, unsweetened liquid made by soaking shredded, fresh coconut with an equal amount of warm milk or water. The mixture is steeped together and then strained, pressing out as much of the fat and flavor from the coconut meat as possible. You can make coconut milk yourself or purchase it canned from most well-stocked grocery stores or Asian markets.

### CREAM OF COCONUT

This thick, creamy, coconut syrup, made from ground coconut and lots of sugar, is popular in baking and as a flavoring in tropical drinks. Coco Lopez is a well-known brand. Since it

## CRACKING COCONUTS

tends to separate, remove all the contents from the can and whisk smooth before using.

### DESICCATED COCONUT

Desiccated coconut, sometimes called macaroon coconut, is dry and fluffy, very finely ground, and similar in texture to cornmeal. It is available sweetened and unsweetened. Often used in candy making or for sweets when a subtle, less obvious coconut flavor, and drier texture, is desired. Desiccated coconut is very popular in desserts and confections from England, New Zealand, and Australia.

### FRESH COCONUT

Available year-round, coconuts are at their peak from October through December. When shopping for a coconut, choose one that is dark brown, with a shaggy, hairy coat. It should feel heavy in your hand, and when you shake it, it should make a lively, sloshing sound indicating it is fresh and full of juice.

The coconut has three "eyes" or dark spots at one end, and a slightly pointed tip at the other. Hold the coconut in one hand, over the sink, with the three eyes facing toward you. Use a hammer, or the back of a heavy cleaver (I have also used a heavy meat mallet) to strike the coconut firmly in the middle. Give the coconut repeated firm taps with the hammer around its equator until it breaks in two and releases the coconut juice.

Place the coconut halves on a cutting board. Use a blunt-edged table knife to carefully pry the meat from the shell by inserting the knife blade between the coconut meat and the shell and giving it a firm twist. The meat may come loose from the shell in more than one piece.

Use a vegetable peeler or paring knife to scrape the papery brown skin from the coconut meat. Rinse the pieces of coconut under cold running water. Grate the coconut in one of three ways:

1. Use a box grater to shred the large chunks of coconut against the smallest holes of the grater, turning the pieces often to avoid cutting your fingers against the grater's sharp holes.

2. Fit a food processor with the metal chopping blade. Cut the coconut into ½-inch pieces. With the motor running, process the coconut, a few pieces at a time, until it is finely grated and almost fluffy, stopping the machine occasionally to scrape down the sides of the bowl.

3. My favorite method is to use a microplane grater (see page 11). Grating coconut with this tool makes heaps of delicate coconut snow. Watch your fingers as with the box grater.

One fresh coconut yields 3 to 4 cups grated coconut.

### SWEETENED SHREDDED COCONUT

This is the most readily available prepared coconut and is found in 8-ounce and 16-ounce bags in most grocery stores.

### UNSWEETENED FLAKED COCONUT

Available in natural- and health-food stores, flaked coconut has wider, sturdier shards than shredded, and can sometimes be substituted for fresh, if that is not available.

I love the sharp sweetness and the startling deep pink of Ruby Red grapefruit. Combined with a little lemon juice and tangerine zest, their clear, tangy juices make a delicious citrus mousse. You can use a fork, but these phyllo ruffles make sturdy little crisps to scoop up the tart cream, so use your fingers and dig in.

# Sweet Pink Grapefruit–Tangerine Mousse with Crispy Phyllo Ruffles SERVES 6

**FOR THE GRAPEFRUIT-TANGERINE CURD:**

3 LARGE EGGS

3 LARGE EGG YOLKS

1/2 CUP FRESHLY SQUEEZED PINK GRAPEFRUIT JUICE

2 TABLESPOONS FRESHLY SQUEEZED LEMON JUICE

GRATED ZEST AND JUICE OF 1 TANGERINE

1 CUP GRANULATED SUGAR

PINCH OF SALT

6 TABLESPOONS UNSALTED BUTTER, AT ROOM TEMPERATURE

1 OR 2 DROPS PINK FOOD COLORING

**FOR THE PHYLLO RUFFLES:**

6 SHEETS PHYLLO DOUGH, THAWED (SEE PAGE 98)

6 TABLESPOONS UNSALTED BUTTER, MELTED

3/4 CUP CONFECTIONERS' SUGAR

1 CUP HEAVY CREAM

1/3 CUP FINELY CHOPPED PISTACHIOS

FRESH RASPBERRIES FOR SERVING (OPTIONAL)

CONFECTIONERS' SUGAR FOR DUSTING

**TO MAKE THE GRAPEFRUIT-TANGERINE CURD:** Combine the eggs and egg yolks in a small bowl and beat well with a fork or small whisk. Combine the eggs with the grapefruit juice, lemon juice, tangerine zest and juice, granulated sugar, and salt in the top pan of a double boiler. Whisk well, then whisk in the butter. (The mixture will look lumpy and curdled at this time—don't worry, as the butter melts the mixture will smooth out as it cooks and thickens.) If a double boiler isn't available, place the ingredients in a stainless-steel bowl and place the bowl over a large saucepan of simmering water. Stir the grapefruit mixture constantly over simmering water until the mixture smooths out and thickens enough to thickly coat the back of a wooden spoon. Do not let the mixture boil, or it will curdle. Remove the curd from the heat and whisk in 1 or 2 drops pink food coloring to give it a pale, blush pink color.

**PRESS THE GRAPEFRUIT CURD THROUGH A FINE-MESH SIEVE INTO A CLEAN BOWL.** Cover the warm grapefruit curd with plastic wrap, pressing it onto the surface of the curd to prevent a skin from forming. Refrigerate until very cold, at least 3 hours or up to 24 hours.

**WHILE THE GRAPEFRUIT CURD IS CHILLING, MAKE THE PHYLLO RUFFLES:** Preheat the oven to 375°F. Line a baking sheet with parchment paper.

CONTINUED

*"The kitchen is my favorite room. It's easy to keep clean. I have a secret recipe for toasted tangerine."*
—FROM MOSS PILLOWS, BY ROSEMARY WELLS

80

CONTINUED

**LAY 1 SHEET OF PHYLLO DOUGH ON A FLAT SURFACE.** Lightly brush the phyllo with melted butter, working from the edges toward the center. Spoon the confectioners' sugar into a fine-mesh sieve and dust the phyllo generously with sugar. Layer 2 more sheets of phyllo over the first, buttering and dusting with more confectioners' sugar. Cut the layered phyllo lengthwise into two 4½-inch-wide strips. Cut each strip into 3 equal pieces. Take each square of phyllo and pinch it together loosely toward the center to form little ruffled accordion pleats that meet in the center (like a little farfalle, or bow-tie, pasta). Repeat with the remaining 5 squares. Place the phyllo ruffles on the prepared pan and bake for 6 to 7 minutes, until phyllo is crisp and golden. Repeat this process with the remaining 3 sheets of phyllo dough for a total of 12 phyllo ruffles. (The phyllo ruffles can be stored in an airtight container for 1 to 2 days.)

**TO FINISH THE MOUSSE,** beat the heavy cream in a chilled bowl with an electric mixer set at medium speed until soft peaks form. Using a large rubber spatula, fold the whipped cream into the grapefruit-tangerine curd until smooth and well combined.

**TO ASSEMBLE THE PASTRIES,** place a phyllo ruffle on a individual dessert plate and top with approximately ⅓ cup of the grapefruit-tangerine mousse. Top with a second phyllo ruffle. Top the second phyllo ruffle with another ⅓ cup mousse. Top with chopped pistachios and a few fresh raspberries (if desired), and dust with confectioners' sugar. Repeat with the remaining 5 servings.

Old-fashioned English desserts like trifle epitomize the comfortable, gooey world laid out in this book. Espresso, chocolate, and hazelnut are a classic combination and a good place, I thought, to start hunting for big flavor ideas for this rich pudding. The best part about this dessert is that you can make it in stages—the cake one day, the custard another, and the whipped cream right before you serve it. This is a big, grand, beautiful dessert, deserving of a birthday or other festive celebration. It will satisfy the appetite of the most ravenous nut-loving sweet tooth.

# Mocha Hazelnut Trifle with Kahlúa Whipped Cream SERVES 6 TO 8

2 LOAVES (EACH 81/2 BY 41/2-INCHES) HAZELNUT POUND CAKE (PAGE 105)

1 JAR NUTELLA

1/2 CUP HAZELNUT-FLAVORED SYRUP SUCH AS TORANI

1 SHOT STRONG ESPRESSO, OR 1 TEASPOON INSTANT ESPRESSO POWDER DISSOLVED IN 2 TABLE-SPOONS HOT WATER

3 OR 4 TABLESPOONS FRANGELICO OR OTHER HAZELNUT LIQUEUR

FRANGELICO CUSTARD (FACING PAGE)

**FOR THE KAHLÚA WHIPPED CREAM:**

2 CUPS HEAVY CREAM

1 TEASPOON INSTANT ESPRESSO POWDER

1/3 CUP CONFECTIONERS' SUGAR

2 TO 4 TABLESPOONS KAHLÚA

1/2 CUP FINELY CHOPPED, TOASTED HAZELNUTS (SEE PAGE 89)

CUT EACH POUND CAKE CROSSWISE INTO ABOUT 8 SLICES, each approximately 1 inch thick, and make sandwiches with the cake slices using the Nutella as filling. Cut each sandwich into 4 squares and arrange them over the bottom of a large shallow glass bowl or trifle dish.

IN A BOWL, stir the hazelnut syrup, espresso, and Frangelico together and drizzle it over the cake. Allow the syrup to soak into the cake while you make the Frangelico Custard. Carefully spoon the cooled custard over the cake. Press a large piece of plastic wrap over the surface of the custard to prevent a skin from forming and refrigerate the trifle until ready to serve, at least 3 hours but preferably overnight.

RIGHT BEFORE SERVING, MAKE THE KAHLÚA WHIPPED CREAM: Combine the cream, espresso powder, confectioners' sugar, and 2 tablespoons Kahlúa in a bowl and beat with an electric mixer set at medium speed until soft peaks form. Taste the cream, and if a more pronounced flavor is desired, fold in up to 2 more table-spoons of the Kahlúa. Spread the cream in great, swirling billows over the cold custard. Scatter the chopped hazelnuts over the top and serve.

# Frangelico Custard MAKES ABOUT 4 CUPS CUSTARD

**This creamy, hazelnut-scented custard will meld into the pound cake more readily if it is chilled overnight to allow all the flavors to blend together.**

2 CUPS HEAVY CREAM

1 1/2 CUPS WHOLE MILK

1 CUP SUGAR

9 EGG YOLKS

6 TABLESPOONS ALL-PURPOSE FLOUR

PINCH OF SALT

2 TEASPOONS PURE VANILLA EXTRACT

3 TABLESPOONS UNSALTED BUTTER, AT ROOM TEMPERATURE

4 TABLESPOONS FRANGELICO

COMBINE THE CREAM AND MILK WITH 1/2 CUP SUGAR IN A HEAVY-BOTTOMED SAUCEPAN OVER MEDIUM HEAT AND COOK, stirring to dissolve the sugar. Heat just until the mixture is about to boil (when bubbles start to form around the edge of the pan). Remove from the heat.

IN A LARGE BOWL, whisk the egg yolks together with the remaining 1/2 cup sugar until light and creamy. Whisk the flour into the egg yolks until smooth.

WHISK THE HOT CREAM MIXTURE INTO THE EGG MIXTURE, 1/4 cup at a time, to temper it. Strain the mixture back into the saucepan. Cook over medium heat, stirring constantly, until the custard thickens and comes to a slow boil. Reduce heat to medium-low and continue cooking, whisking continuously, for 1 minute. Remove from the heat and pour the custard through a fine-mesh sieve into a clean bowl. Stir in the salt, vanilla, butter, and Frangelico until smooth. Place the bowl in the freezer and cool, stirring occasionally, for 10 to 15 minutes (the custard should no longer be steaming). At this point, the custard is ready to be used for the trifle.

3

# COOKIES, CAKES & PIES

*Oh My!*

I have traveled far
and wide, but I have never tasted
anything as perfect as a fat, warm chocolate
chip cookie, chunky, with the soft crunch of
slightly astringent walnuts and gooey with chunks
of melting chocolate.

Or maybe perfection lies in a thick bar of buttery shortbread, barely golden and seething with a gooey center of melted caramel. How about a tall, all-American layer cake, sitting high and proud, with as much delectable frosting as moist cake; or a simple, elegant pound cake, fragrant with almonds, with a dense velvety texture and a crumb as fine as silk? I just can't decide. Are you more interested in pie? Imagine a flaky crust holding apple slices snuggled in a warm cinnamon-speckled syrup under a crumbled crown of crisped brown sugar, or tender macadamia nuts jostled and bumping together in a chewy cream of butterscotch and bourbon.

They are all here, waiting for you. Perfection is truly in the eye of the beholder, so if you can't decide between a cookie, a cake, or a pie—don't. Dive into these pages and try them all.

Peters' Bakery is an institution in San Jose, California, where I grew up. Tony Peters opened his family bakery in 1936, and for seventy years he and his family have kept their bakery cases filled with homemade goodies. Their date bars are heavenly, and a family favorite. They even survived a long trek to Bahrain in a care package for my husband. Nancy Peters, Tony's daughter-in-law, just laughed when I asked for the secret recipe, so I developed my own version and, if not exact, it captures the essence of their delicious little bars. Desiccated coconut may seem unusual, but its dry, crumbly texture and subtle coconut flavor balance the creamy, caramelized sweetness of the date filling.

# Chewy Date Bars MAKES 24 BARS

1 POUND (4 STICKS) UNSALTED BUTTER, AT ROOM TEMPERATURE

1 CUP GRANULATED SUGAR

1½ CUPS CONFECTIONERS' SUGAR

2 TEASPOONS PURE VANILLA EXTRACT

1½ TEASPOONS SALT

4 CUPS UNBLEACHED ALL-PURPOSE FLOUR

2 TEASPOONS BAKING POWDER

1⅓ CUPS DESICCATED (OR MACAROON) COCONUT (SEE PAGE 78)

**FOR THE DATE FILLING:**

1 POUND DATES, PREFERABLY MEDJOOL, PITTED AND COARSELY CHOPPED

1½ CUPS WATER

¼ CUP GRANULATED SUGAR

COMBINE THE BUTTER AND SUGARS IN A LARGE BOWL. With an electric mixer set at medium speed, beat the butter and sugars together until creamy. Add the vanilla and salt and beat to combine. Beat in the flour, baking powder, and 1 cup of the coconut just until a soft dough forms.

SPRAY A 9-BY-13-INCH BAKING PAN WITH NONSTICK COOKING SPRAY. Press one-third of the dough into the pan to form a bottom crust. Wrap the remaining dough in plastic wrap and refrigerate until firm, at least 30 minutes.

MEANWHILE, MAKE THE FILLING: Combine the dates, water, and granulated sugar in a heavy-bottomed saucepan over medium heat. Cover the pan and cook the dates, stirring occasionally, until they are very soft and have turned into a glossy brown mass, 10 to 15 minutes. There still may be chunks of dates in the mixture. Remove from the heat and let cool slightly. Transfer the date mixture to a food processor fitted with a metal blade and, using short pulses, grind the dates to a fine paste.

POSITION A RACK IN THE MIDDLE OF THE OVEN AND PREHEAT TO 325°F. Bake the bottom crust until firm and just beginning to turn golden around the edges of the pan, 20 to 25 minutes. Let cool slightly. Spread the date filling evenly over the crust. Crumble the remaining dough over the date filling to form a pebbly, crumbled topping.

RETURN THE PAN TO THE OVEN AND CONTINUE BAKING UNTIL THE TOPPING IS FIRM AND CRISP AND JUST BEGINNING TO COLOR, about 30 minutes. Remove the pan from the oven and sprinkle with the remaining ⅓ cup coconut. Let cool to room temperature on a wire rack. Using a sharp knife, cut into 24 bars and serve. These bars are great "keepers" and can be stored in a tightly covered container for up to 1 week, or frozen for up to 1 month.

When I was growing up, Baskin-Robbins Ice Cream Parlor was the pièce de résistance in cool dessert spots. My dad always let us get a triple scoop, which felt very indulgent, and my brothers and I, after much deliberation, almost always chose the same flavors every time. I loved Nutty Coconut: a creamy vanilla-coconut custard chock-full of walnuts, pecans, and almonds, and more flaked coconut. It is still one of my favorite combinations—in ice cream, or here, as a chewy, sweet cookie. These are for true coconut lovers only.

# Nutty Coconut Macaroons MAKES ABOUT 24 COOKIES

1 PACKAGE (14 OUNCES) SWEETENED SHREDDED COCONUT

1/2 CUP CHOPPED PECANS, TOASTED (SEE FACING PAGE) AND COOLED

1/2 CUP CHOPPED RAW ALMONDS, TOASTED (SEE FACING PAGE) AND COOLED

1/2 CUP FINELY CHOPPED WALNUTS, TOASTED AND COOLED (OPTIONAL; SEE FACING PAGE)

2 TABLESPOONS ALL-PURPOSE FLOUR

1 CAN (14 OUNCES) SWEETENED CONDENSED MILK

4 TABLESPOONS CREAM OF COCONUT (SEE PAGE 78)

PINCH OF SALT

1 TEASPOON PURE VANILLA EXTRACT

1/2 TEASPOON PURE ALMOND EXTRACT

2 EGG WHITES, WHIPPED TO STIFF PEAKS

POSITION A RACK IN THE MIDDLE OF THE OVEN AND PREHEAT TO 350°F. Line 2 baking sheets with parchment paper.

IN A BOWL, combine the coconut, pecans, almonds, and walnuts with the flour, tossing to evenly coat the strands of coconut with flour and untangle any clumps, if necessary. Stir in the sweetened condensed milk, cream of coconut, salt, and vanilla and almond extracts. The dough will be very sticky.

CAREFULLY FOLD IN THE BEATEN EGG WHITES. Drop the batter onto the prepared baking sheets using a 2-ounce ice-cream scoop or 1/4-cup measuring cup.

BAKE UNTIL GOLDEN BROWN, 20 to 25 minutes. Let cool completely before serving. These cookies are best served the day they are made, but can be stored, tightly covered, for up to 2 days before they start getting too sticky.

I am a nut fiend, and I think every sticky, chewy dessert becomes more flavorsome and luxuriously delicious with the judicious use of a few fat, sweet nuts. Almonds, hazelnuts, pecans, walnuts, cashews, macadamia nuts, and pistachios are among my favorites. Here are a few tips for handling and storing nuts to make your sweet treats even more delicious.

Buy shelled nuts in the largest pieces you can, and then chop and toast them as needed. Macadamia nuts, almonds, cashews, and pistachios are available as whole nuts, and walnuts and pecans are available in halves.

Nuts tend to go rancid quickly, so I like to store mine, well wrapped in self-sealing plastic bags, in the freezer. A large bag of shelled nuts will stay fresh for up to 6 months this way.

## TOASTING NUTS

To release the maximum amount of nutty goodness, nuts really should be toasted before they are added to most recipes. Nuts should be chopped to the desired size before, not after, toasting. This will help release their oils and maximize their flavor. Cool the nuts, unless specified otherwise, before adding to your dish. To toast nuts, place chopped nuts on an ungreased baking sheet and bake in a preheated 350°F oven until warm and fragrant, 6 to 10 minutes, depending on the type. Stir the nuts once or twice while they are baking to check that they don't burn.

## SKINNING NUTS

Pistachios and hazelnuts have tenacious, bitter, papery skins that need to be removed before the nuts' sweetness and flavor can be appreciated. Toast hazelnuts or pistachios by placing the shelled nuts in a single layer on a baking sheet and bake in a preheated 350°F oven, stirring occasionally to make sure they don't burn, until warm and fragrant, 8 to 10 minutes. Transfer the nuts to a clean kitchen towel with a coarse weave and rub them vigorously to remove the skins.

## BLANCHING NUTS

Raw almonds can be enjoyed with the skin, but if a more delicate flavor and color is desired, the skin can also be removed. Toasting raw almonds only seems to make their skins hug the nutmeat even tighter, so almonds must be blanched to remove

their skins. Bring a saucepan three-fourths full of water to a boil. Stir in the shelled raw almonds. Cover the pan and remove from the heat. Let the nuts stand in the hot water for 2 to 3 minutes. Drain the water and, while the nuts are wet, pop the nuts out of their loose skins. If the almonds seem too soft after their soaking, dry them and place in a single layer on a metal baking sheet. Bake in a preheated 350°F oven for 2 minutes to restore their crunch. Do not allow blanched nuts to brown.

## NUT FLOUR

You can often find almond and hazelnut "meal" or "flour" in health-food or whole-food markets or from many mail-order sources. Nut flours have a fine, powdery texture, and are a delicious addition to many cakes and other confections in place of part of the flour, giving the recipe an added depth of flavor and texture.

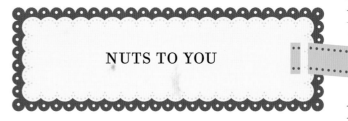

## NUTS TO YOU

If you want to make your own nut meal or flour, toast the nuts as directed and let cool. Grind them in a small food processor fitted with the metal chopping blade or in a spice grinder. The spice grinder yields the finest, fluffiest nut flour, but you can only make a small amount at a time. To prevent your nuts from turning from flour to butter in a food processor, add a tablespoon or two of confectioners' sugar or all-purpose flour halfway through the grinding process. This will buffer the nuts and prevent them from turning to an oily paste before they are ground as finely as they need to be for a proper nut flour.

These thick, buttery bars are my idea of heaven, and are my favorite cookie, bar none. Something magical happens with shortbread's simple combination of butter, sugar, and flour. I consider shortbread one of the Super Foods—right up there with salmon and flaxseeds and tofu (if you factor in happiness as one of its health benefits). This version includes almonds and tangy blackberry jam to harmonize with the shortbread's sweet simplicity. Raspberry or apricot jam would make a tasty substitute.

# Blackberry Jamble
## Shortbread Bars MAKES 15 LARGE OR 30 SMALL BARS

1 POUND (4 STICKS) UNSALTED BUTTER, AT ROOM TEMPERATURE

1 CUP FIRMLY PACKED LIGHT BROWN SUGAR

1 CUP GRANULATED SUGAR

2 TEASPOONS PURE VANILLA EXTRACT

1 TEASPOON SALT

3 3/4 CUPS UNBLEACHED ALL-PURPOSE FLOUR

1 CUP ALMOND FLOUR OR VERY FINELY GROUND ALMONDS (SEE PAGE 89)

1 1/2 CUPS BLACKBERRY PRESERVES

1/2 CUP CHOPPED ALMONDS

CONFECTIONERS' SUGAR FOR DUSTING

COMBINE THE BUTTER AND SUGARS IN A LARGE BOWL. Using an electric mixer set at medium-low speed, beat until creamy. Add the vanilla and salt and beat until combined.

BEAT THE ALL-PURPOSE AND ALMOND FLOURS INTO THE BUTTER MIXTURE ON LOW SPEED, just until a smooth, soft dough forms.

SPRAY A 9-BY-13-INCH BAKING PAN WITH NONSTICK COOKING SPRAY AND PRESS ONE-THIRD OF THE DOUGH EVENLY INTO THE PAN TO FORM A BOTTOM CRUST. Wrap the remaining dough in plastic wrap and refrigerate until very cold and firm, at least 30 minutes.

POSITION A RACK IN THE MIDDLE OF THE OVEN AND PREHEAT TO 325°F.

BAKE THE BOTTOM CRUST UNTIL IT IS FIRM AND JUST BEGINNING TO TURN PALE BROWN AROUND THE EDGES, about 20 minutes. Remove the pan from the oven and spread the preserves evenly over the crust. Crumble the remaining shortbread dough over the jam to form a pebbly, crumbled topping. Sprinkle with the chopped almonds. Return the pan to the oven and continue baking until topping is firm and crisp and lightly golden in color, about 30 minutes. Transfer to a wire rack and let cool to room temperature.

USE A SHARP KNIFE TO CUT BARS EVENLY INTO 15 LARGE SQUARES. Remove the bars from the pan with a metal spatula and, if desired, cut in half on the diagonal to form 30 smaller triangular bars. Dust with confectioners' sugar and serve.

THE BARS WILL KEEP, covered tightly, for about 1 week at room temperature, or in the freezer for up to 1 month.

If you are a sucker for shortbread cookies, you'll swoon over these gooey bars. The chewy caramel sandwiched between the sweet, buttery crispness of the shortbread is a real crowd-pleaser. I love nuts in all my cookies, but if you're nut-averse like my children, leave them out. The dark rum in the caramel filling lends a spirited flavor, but as with the nuts, these bars are equally tasty without it.

# Gooey Caramel Butter Bars

MAKES 15 LARGE OR 30 SMALL BARS

**FOR THE CRUST:**

1 POUND (4 STICKS) UNSALTED BUTTER, AT ROOM TEMPERATURE

1 CUP GRANULATED SUGAR

1 1/2 CUPS CONFECTIONERS' SUGAR, SIFTED

1 TABLESPOON PURE VANILLA EXTRACT

1 TEASPOON SALT

4 CUPS UNBLEACHED ALL-PURPOSE FLOUR

**FOR THE FILLING:**

1 BAG (14 OUNCES) CARAMEL CANDIES (ABOUT 50 INDIVIDUAL CARAMELS), UNWRAPPED

1/3 CUP HEAVY CREAM

1/2 TEASPOON PURE VANILLA EXTRACT

1 TO 2 TABLESPOONS DARK RUM (OPTIONAL)

PINCH OF SALT

1 CUP PECANS, WALNUTS, OR CASHEWS (OPTIONAL)

CONFECTIONERS' SUGAR FOR DUSTING (OPTIONAL)

TO MAKE THE CRUST: In a large bowl, combine the butter and sugars. Using an electric mixer set at medium speed, beat together until creamy. Add the vanilla and salt and beat until combined. Sift the flour into the butter mixture and beat on low speed until a smooth, soft dough forms.

SPRAY A 9-BY-13-INCH BAKING PAN LIGHTLY WITH NONSTICK COOKING SPRAY. Press one-third of the dough evenly into the pan to form a bottom crust. Pat the remaining dough into a flat disk and wrap in plastic wrap and refrigerate until firm, at least 30 minutes.

POSITION A RACK IN THE MIDDLE OF THE OVEN AND PREHEAT TO 325°F. Bake until firm and the edges are a pale golden brown, 20 to 25 minutes. Transfer to a wire rack and let cool.

WHILE THE BOTTOM CRUST IS BAKING AND THE REMAINING DOUGH IS CHILLING, MAKE THE CARAMEL FILLING: Place the unwrapped caramels in a microwave-safe bowl. Add the cream, vanilla, rum (if using), and salt. Microwave on high for 1 minute. Remove from the microwave and stir until smooth. If caramels are not completely melted, microwave on high for 30-second intervals, stirring after each interval, until smooth.

SPRINKLE THE NUTS (IF USING) OVER THE BOTTOM CRUST. Pour the caramel filling over the nuts, using a small metal spatula to nudge the filling evenly over the crust. Remove the remaining chilled dough from the refrigerator and crumble it evenly over the caramel. Return the pan to the oven and bake until the filling is bubbly and the crumbled shortbread topping is firm and lightly golden, about 30 minutes. Transfer to a wire rack and let cool completely.

USE A SHARP KNIFE TO CUT THE BARS EVENLY INTO 15 LARGE SQUARES. Remove the bars from the pan with a metal spatula and, if desired, cut in half on the diagonal to form 30 triangular bars. Dust with confectioners' sugar, if desired.

THE BARS WILL KEEP, covered tightly at room temperature, for about 1 week, or in the freezer for up to 1 month.

There's nothing dainty or subtle in these big, bodacious butterscotch bars. Sometimes less is more, but not with these bold, chunky beauties. They sport an audaciously extreme mixture of pecans, almonds, and walnuts; chewy coconut; and big chunks of sweet toffee and chocolate chips. Delish!

# Big Blondes

MAKES 15 LARGE OR 30 SMALL BARS

1 CUP (2 STICKS) UNSALTED BUTTER

3 CUPS FIRMLY PACKED DARK BROWN SUGAR

4 LARGE EGGS

1 TABLESPOON PURE VANILLA EXTRACT

1 TEASPOON SALT

2 CUPS UNBLEACHED ALL-PURPOSE FLOUR

3/4 TEASPOON BAKING POWDER

1 CUP PECAN HALVES, TOASTED (SEE PAGE 89)

1 CUP WALNUT HALVES, TOASTED (SEE PAGE 89)

1 CUP WHOLE RAW ALMONDS, COARSELY CHOPPED AND TOASTED (SEE PAGE 89)

1 CUP SWEETENED SHREDDED COCONUT (SEE PAGE 78)

4 OR 5 FULL-SIZE (1.4 OUNCES) TOFFEE CANDY BARS SUCH AS HEATH, VERY COARSELY CHOPPED

1 CUP WHITE CHOCOLATE CHIPS

1 CUP SEMISWEET CHOCOLATE CHIPS

POSITION A RACK IN THE MIDDLE OF THE OVEN AND PREHEAT TO 350°F. Spray a 9-by-13-inch baking pan with nonstick cooking spray.

MELT THE BUTTER AND BROWN SUGAR TOGETHER IN A LARGE HEAVY-BOTTOMED SAUCEPAN OVER MEDIUM HEAT. Cook, stirring constantly, until the butter and sugar are blended and completely melted and starting to bubble gently. Remove the pan from heat and let the mixture cool slightly.

IN A BOWL, whisk together the eggs, vanilla, and salt. Slowly whisk the cooled butter and sugar mixture into the eggs just until combined. Whisk in the flour and baking powder to form a loose batter. (Make sure the batter is cool before stirring in the remaining ingredients; otherwise the chocolate will start to melt before the bars are baked.)

STIR THE NUTS, coconut, toffee chunks, and chocolate chips into the cooled batter. Pour the batter into the prepared pan and smooth the top with a spatula. Bake until the top is shiny and slightly crackled and feels firm to the touch, 30 to 35 minutes. A wooden skewer inserted into the batter should come out with moist crumbs clinging to it. Let cool on a wire rack to room temperature, then cut into bars and serve.

I learned to make these rugged, chewy, palm-size cookies, called Ranger Cookies, the summer I worked at Mountain Meadow Ranch in California's Trinity Alps. They are bag-lunch favorites with the avid hikers, backpackers, nature photographers, and families who made the long, bone-rattling trek up dusty Coffee Creek Road to visit the mountain resort every summer. Mountain Meadow cooks have been baking these tasty cookies for years, and everyone has fiddled with the original recipe, leaving their own particular imprint on its flavor. My friend, and Mountain Meadow's summer kitchen manager, Vicki Villarreal's extra-chewy version is a favorite. I've loaded mine with extra chocolate and nuts. The classic recipe calls for Rice Krispies, but crisped rice flakes cereal (like Special K) adds a delicate crackle. It's a fun recipe to play with and, frankly, any variation you come up with will be delicious.

# Everything-but-the-Kitchen-Sink Cookies

MAKES 4 TO 5 DOZEN COOKIES

3 CUPS WALNUT OR PECAN HALVES

2 CUPS (4 STICKS) UNSALTED BUTTER, AT ROOM TEMPERATURE

2 CUPS FIRMLY PACKED DARK BROWN SUGAR

2 CUPS GRANULATED SUGAR

4 LARGE EGGS

4 TEASPOONS PURE VANILLA EXTRACT

4 CUPS UNBLEACHED ALL-PURPOSE FLOUR

1 TABLESPOON BAKING SODA

1 1/2 TEASPOONS SALT

4 CUPS CRISPED RICE OR CRISPY RICE FLAKES CEREAL SUCH AS RICE KRISPIES OR SPECIAL K

2 CUPS SWEETENED SHREDDED COCONUT (SEE PAGE 78)

4 CUPS OLD-FASHIONED ROLLED OATS

3 CUPS SEMISWEET CHOCOLATE CHIPS

POSITION A RACK IN THE MIDDLE OF THE OVEN AND PREHEAT TO 350°F.

PLACE THE WALNUT HALVES ON A BAKING SHEET AND TOAST, stirring occasionally, until browned and fragrant, 6 to 10 minutes. Transfer to a plate and let cool completely.

IN A LARGE BOWL, using an electric mixer set at medium speed, cream together the butter and sugars until light and fluffy, about 2 minutes. Beat in the eggs, one at a time, beating well after each addition. Beat in the vanilla. Sift together the flour, baking soda, and salt onto a piece of waxed paper. Beat into the butter mixture to form a soft dough.

IN ANOTHER LARGE BOWL, toss together the toasted nuts, rice cereal, coconut, oats, and chocolate chips. Use a large wooden spoon to stir all the dry ingredients into the soft dough. Don't worry about incorporating all these ingredients into the dough—it just takes a little patience, a sturdy wooden spoon, and a strong arm.

SCOOP THE DOUGH INTO 1/4-CUP BALLS (I LIKE TO USE A 2-OUNCE ICE-CREAM SCOOP). Place the cookie dough balls on parchment paper–lined baking sheets at least 2 inches apart. Flatten each dough ball slightly with two wet fingers to keep the cookies from puffing up too much as they bake. Bake until the edges of the cookie are light brown and crisp but the centers of the cookie are still soft and a little puffy, 12 to 15 minutes.

LET THE COOKIES COOL SLIGHTLY ON THE BAKING SHEET BEFORE REMOVING THEM WITH A SPATULA TO A WIRE RACK TO FINISH COOLING.

These glossy, crisp cookies replace the classic addition of flaked almonds with chewy-sweet oatmeal. Sandwich them with peanut butter–caramel for an all-American take on a French classic.

# Crispy Oatmeal Florentines with Peanut Butter–Caramel Filling

MAKES 12 TO 15 COOKIE SANDWICHES

2/3 CUP SUGAR

1/2 CUP (1 STICK) UNSALTED BUTTER

1/3 CUP LIGHT CORN SYRUP

1 1/4 CUPS OLD-FASHIONED ROLLED OATS

1 CUP CAKE FLOUR, SIFTED AND THEN MEASURED

PINCH OF SALT

**FOR THE PEANUT BUTTER–CARAMEL FILLING:**

7 OUNCES CARAMEL CANDIES (ABOUT 25 INDIVIDUAL CANDIES), UNWRAPPED

3 TABLESPOONS CREAMY PEANUT BUTTER

1/2 TEASPOON PURE VANILLA EXTRACT

IN A HEAVY-BOTTOMED SAUCEPAN OVER MEDIUM HEAT, combine the sugar, butter, and corn syrup. Cook, stirring constantly, until the butter is melted and the mixture is smooth and combined.

INCREASE THE HEAT TO HIGH AND BRING THE MIXTURE TO A BOIL. Remove from the heat and stir in the oats. Add the flour and salt and stir until smooth. Transfer the batter to a bowl to cool. Cover the bowl and refrigerate the batter for at least 1 hour. At this point the batter can be refrigerated for up to 1 week. The batter will be very stiff.

POSITION A RACK IN THE MIDDLE OF THE OVEN AND PREHEAT TO 325°F. Line a baking sheet with parchment paper.

ROLL LEVEL TABLESPOONS OF THE BATTER BETWEEN YOUR PALMS TO FORM SMALL BALLS. Place them on the prepared baking sheet at least 3 inches apart. Bake the florentines until they are flat, lacy, and a deep glossy golden brown, 7 to 10 minutes. Transfer to a wire rack and let cool completely on the baking sheet.

TO MAKE THE FILLING: Combine the caramels, peanut butter, and vanilla in a microwave-safe bowl. Microwave on high for 1 minute. Remove and stir the mixture until smooth and combined. If the caramels are not completely melted, continue to microwave for 30-second intervals and stir until smooth.

USE A METAL SPATULA TO REMOVE A COOLED FLORENTINE FROM THE BAKING SHEET. Spread 2 or 3 teaspoons of the peanut butter–caramel filling over the bottom of the cookie and sandwich it with a second florentine.

THE FLORENTINES WILL KEEP, tightly covered, for up to 2 days. After this time they will start to lose their crispness and get a little soft and chewy.

Financiers are dense, chewy little rectangular cake bars named for the glittering gold bricks they resemble. Here, stuffed with zesty pea-green pistachios and a zing of lemon, they really shine.

# Chewy Lemon-Pistachio Financiers

MAKES ABOUT 2 DOZEN BARS

1/2 CUP GROUND BLANCHED SLIVERED ALMONDS (SEE PAGE 89)

1 CUP GROUND SHELLED AND TOASTED UNSALTED PISTACHIOS (SEE PAGE 89)

1 1/2 CUPS CONFECTIONERS' SUGAR, PLUS EXTRA FOR DUSTING (OPTIONAL)

2/3 CUP GRANULATED SUGAR

ZEST OF 2 LEMONS

8 LARGE EGG WHITES

1 TEASPOON PURE VANILLA EXTRACT

3/4 CUP UNBLEACHED ALL-PURPOSE FLOUR

1/4 TEASPOON SALT

1 CUP (2 STICKS) UNSALTED BUTTER, MELTED

COMBINE THE GROUND ALMONDS, pistachios, and 1 1/2 cups confectioners' sugar in a food processor. Grind the nuts and sugar together until the mixture is very fine and powdery.

TRANSFER THE NUT MIXTURE TO A LARGE BOWL AND STIR IN THE GRANULATED SUGAR, lemon zest, egg whites, and vanilla just until smooth and combined. Sift the flour and salt together onto a piece of waxed paper and gently fold into the batter.

CAREFULLY STIR THE MELTED BUTTER INTO THE BATTER. Cover the bowl with plastic wrap and refrigerate until the batter is very cold and firm, at least 1 hour and up to 24 hours.

POSITION A RACK IN THE MIDDLE OF THE OVEN AND PREHEAT THE OVEN TO 450°F. Spray the molds of a financier pan, cups of a mini muffin or muffin-top pan, or small decorative molds with nonstick cooking spray. Fill the molds three-fourths full of batter. Place the filled pan or other pans on a baking sheet and bake for 7 minutes. Reduce the oven temperature to 400°F and continue baking until firm and golden, about 7 minutes longer. Remove the financiers from the oven, unmold immediately onto a wire rack, and let cool completely. Dust with confectioners' sugar, if desired.

What are they? A cookie? A candy? These chewy little pastry bites defy categorization. Gooey, decadent, and very addictive, they have it all. I created these little treats for my book *Phyllo,* and I think they bear repeating in a book that celebrates all things sweet and sticky.

# Honey Caramel-Pecan Phyllo Slices

MAKES ABOUT 4 DOZEN

**FOR THE CARAMEL:**

3/4 CUP MILD HONEY

2 CUPS HEAVY CREAM

1 1/4 CUPS GRANULATED SUGAR

1/4 TEASPOON SALT

2 TEASPOONS PURE VANILLA EXTRACT

12 OUNCES PECANS, COARSELY CHOPPED

FORTY-EIGHT 9-BY-13-INCH SHEETS PHYLLO DOUGH (ABOUT 1 1/2 LBS), THAWED (SEE PAGE 98)

1 CUP (2 STICKS) BUTTER, MELTED

1 1/4 CUPS GRANULATED SUGAR

**TO MAKE THE CARAMEL:** In a heavy-bottomed saucepan over low heat, combine the honey, cream, sugar, and salt. Cook until the sugar is dissolved. Increase the heat to high and bring the mixture to a gentle boil. Cook, stirring occasionally, until the mixture becomes thick and syrupy and turns a warm, caramel brown, 5 to 7 minutes. The syrup should reach the soft-ball stage (see page 154) and register 240°F on a candy thermometer. Remove from the heat and stir in the vanilla and pecans.

**POUR THE CARAMEL INTO AN OILED BOWL.** Let rest until it is cool enough to handle but still malleable. Divide the caramel into 12 equal portions. Using your hands, shape each portion into a long rope about 8 inches long and 3/4 inch thick. Let the caramel ropes cool completely on a baking sheet. The caramel will firm up as it cools.

**PREHEAT THE OVEN TO 375°F.** Line 2 baking sheets with parchment paper.

**LAY 1 SHEET OF PHYLLO DOUGH FLAT ON A WORK SURFACE.** Brush lightly with melted butter, working from the edges to the center. Sprinkle with 2 tablespoons of the sugar. Layer 3 more sheets of phyllo dough over the first, brushing with butter and sprinkling each with 2 tablespoons sugar. Lay one caramel rope down the long side of the phyllo about 1 inch from the edge. Fold the edges of the phyllo over the caramel rope and roll up like a jelly roll, completely encasing the caramel in phyllo. Brush the pastry with more butter and sprinkle with sugar. Lay the pastry, seam-side down, on the parchment paper–lined baking sheet. Repeat this process with the remaining phyllo dough and caramel ropes for a total of 12 long pastries. Arrange 4 on each prepared baking sheet and set aside the remaining 4 on a clean work surface.

**BAKE UNTIL THE PHYLLO IS CRISP AND GOLDEN BROWN,** 15 to 20 minutes. Transfer the rolls to wire racks and let cool completely. The caramel inside the pastries will soften as it bakes and firm up again as it cools. Bake the remaining 4 pastries on a clean parchment paper–lined baking sheet. Slice them on the diagonal into 1 1/2- to 2-inch-wide pieces when completely cool.

Phyllo (from *phyllon*, the Greek word meaning "leaf") is tissue-paper-thin sheets of pastry dough made from flour, water, and a tiny bit of oil. Sweet and savory fillings are encased in many buttered layers of phyllo, yielding incomparably light, crisp, and flaky pastries. The exact origins of phyllo, called *yufka* by the Turks, is still debated, but this versatile pastry has been popular in Greece and Turkey and throughout the Middle East and parts of Eastern Europe for centuries. Hungarians learned to make strudel dough (very similar to phyllo dough) from the Turks in the 1500s.

Although it is possible to make phyllo dough yourself, it is becoming a lost art. Excellent commercial phyllo dough is readily available fresh and frozen. If you follow these simple rules, working with phyllo dough should be a breeze.

### THAW THE PHYLLO

Phyllo is available in 1-pound boxes, in either 9-by-13-inch or 14-by-18-inch sheets. Phyllo dough needs to be completely thawed before using or the sheets will stick together or crack. It also needs to thaw slowly, for at least 24 hours in the refrigerator. This slow thaw will allow the phyllo sheets to slowly separate from each other and prevent them from sticking together. Bring the phyllo to room temperature by sitting it on the kitchen counter for 2 hours before you even open the box.

## PHYLLO FACTS

## BE ORGANIZED

When working with phyllo, organization is the key to success. Make sure you have your filling prepared, and the rest of your ingredients and a large, flat, clean work surface ready before you begin. Have the following equipment handy:

- A sharp knife

- A large pastry brush

- A ruler to measure phyllo dough before cutting

- A light cotton dishcloth or paper towels

- Heavy baking sheet(s)

- A large metal spatula

- Melted butter, clarified butter, or oil for brushing the phyllo

## HANDLING

The best advice when working with phyllo: Move quickly! Because the sheets of phyllo are paper-thin and very delicate, they dry out quickly when exposed to air and will crack and crumble, making them impossible to work with. Organization will keep you moving quickly. Remember to take the phone off the hook; phyllo waits for no one, and you shouldn't pause until your pastries are oven or freezer bound.

## COVER THE DOUGH

Unroll only the amount of dough you need and wrap the unused portion in plastic wrap before you begin. Cover the unrolled phyllo with a barely damp cotton dishcloth or damp paper towels to prevent phyllo from drying out while you are working. Remove one layer at a time, keeping the remaining sheets covered. (Once you become more adept with phyllo and your preparation speed increases, you can dispense with covering the dough, since you will move too fast for the dough to dry out!)

## COOL THE FILLING

Make sure your filling is completely prepped and cooled before starting to assemble any phyllo pastry. Fillings that are even slightly warm will wilt the pastry, making breaks or tears more likely.

## BUTTER THE DOUGH

For added flavor and crispness, brush each phyllo sheet lightly with melted butter, clarified butter, or olive oil (the latter for savory pastries). Brush the edges first to keep the phyllo from cracking, then move toward the center of the sheet. Don't drench it with butter, but make sure the dough is evenly and lightly covered before you layer on the next sheet of phyllo. If some sheets tear, don't worry! Simply "glue" it together with some melted butter or oil and keep layering.

## SHAPING

Phyllo can be layered and shaped in many creative ways, from strudels, stuffed triangles, and little purses to larger layered pastries like baklava. Layered sheets of buttered phyllo can be cut into squares or rectangles, then baked flat. Use these little pastries instead of puff pastry for lighter, crisper mille-feuilles. Or press buttered squares of phyllo into muffin tins for easy, feather-light pastry cups perfect for both sweet and savory fillings.

## STORING

Unbaked phyllo pastries can be covered and refrigerated for 24 hours before baking, or wrapped well and frozen for up to 1 month. Both chilled and frozen pastries should go straight from the refrigerator or freezer into a hot oven—thawing makes the pastry soggy.

## BAKING

Brush the outside of the pastry with melted butter or oil to protect it and ensure even browning. If your sweet pastries are sprinkled with sugar, line your baking sheet with parchment paper to prevent pastries from sticking and burning. Bake in a hot 375° to 400°F oven for an extra-crisp, golden brown finish. Leftover pastries can be reheated in a 350°F oven until warm and crisp. Don't reheat pastries in the microwave, as they will become very soggy and unpalatable.

4 TABLESPOONS UNSALTED BUTTER

3/4 CUP FIRMLY PACKED LIGHT BROWN SUGAR

2 RIPE PEARS, PEELED, CORED, AND DICED

1/3 CUP COARSELY CHOPPED WALNUTS

I started cooking school in London, at Le Cordon Bleu, shortly after I got married. Although I had lived in London before, I had forgotten how bitterly cold winters there could get. Our flat had no fireplace, and tall windows let in frigid air even when closed. The first weeks of cooking school introduced me to French technique with a decidedly British flavor, and one of my favorite recipes was a quick, classic gingerbread cake—damp and spicy, with a sticky upside-down glaze coating nuggets of sweet pears and chunks of walnuts. Served warm from the oven, accompanied by a strong, hot cup of Earl Grey tea, this cake helped keep me cozy as the windy rain howled outside.

# Sticky Pear and Walnut Upside-Down Gingerbread SERVES 6

**FOR THE BATTER:**

1 CUP PLUS 1 TABLESPOON ALL-PURPOSE FLOUR

1/2 TEASPOON BAKING SODA

1/4 TEASPOON SALT

2 TEASPOONS CINNAMON

2 TEASPOONS GROUND GINGER

1/4 TEASPOON FRESHLY GRATED NUTMEG

PINCH OF GROUND CLOVES

1 LARGE EGG

3/4 CUP FIRMLY PACKED LIGHT BROWN SUGAR

6 TABLESPOONS DARK UNSULPHERED MOLASSES

1/2 CUP BUTTERMILK

4 TABLESPOONS UNSALTED BUTTER, MELTED

SWEETENED WHIPPED CREAM (PAGE 43) OR SOUR CREAM FOR SERVING (OPTIONAL)

POSITION A RACK IN THE MIDDLE OF THE OVEN AND PREHEAT TO 350°F. Spray an 8-inch round cake pan with nonstick cooking spray.

IN A BOWL, cream the butter and sugar together and spread over the bottom and halfway up the sides of the prepared pan. Sprinkle the pears and walnuts over the bottom of the pan. Set aside.

TO MAKE THE BATTER: Sift the flour, baking soda, salt, and spices into a large bowl. In another bowl, whisk together the egg, brown sugar, molasses, buttermilk, and melted butter. Gradually whisk the wet ingredients into the dry ingredients, whisking only until combined. Carefully pour the batter over the nuts and pears in the pan.

BAKE UNTIL THE TOP OF THE CAKE IS FIRM AND SHINY AND THE SIDES ARE PULLING AWAY SLIGHTLY FROM THE PAN, 35 to 45 minutes. Remove the cake from the oven, place a large serving plate over the top of the cake, and turn it out onto the plate. Remove the cake pan. If any nuts or pears are still stuck to the pan, carefully scrape them—and any of the remaining sweet, sticky sauce—onto the cake, smoothing it out with a knife. Let the cake cool slightly, then cut into wedges. Serve warm, dolloped with whipped cream or sweetened sour cream, if desired.

My mother made a version of these delicious cookies every Christmas when I was young. Simultaneously light and crisp, chewy and chocolatey, with the crunch of walnuts and the sweet tingle of peppermint candy canes, they say "Merry Christmas" with each bite. You can pipe these meringues into kisses, but I like to spoon them, free-form, onto the baking sheets in big, luscious clouds.

# Mama's Merry Christmas Meringues

MAKES 24 MERINGUES

3 LARGE EGG WHITES AT ROOM TEMPERATURE

1/4 TEASPOON CREAM OF TARTAR

PINCH OF SALT

1 TEASPOON PURE VANILLA EXTRACT

3/4 CUP GRANULATED SUGAR

1/2 CUP CONFECTIONERS' SUGAR, SIFTED

1/3 CUP COARSELY CRUSHED PEPPERMINT CANDIES

1/3 CUP FINELY CHOPPED WALNUTS

1/3 CUP MINI SEMISWEET CHOCOLATE CHIPS

POSITION A RACK IN THE MIDDLE SHELF OF THE OVEN AND PLACE A SECOND RACK ON THE TOP SHELF. Preheat the oven to 250°F. Line 2 baking sheets with parchment paper.

IN A LARGE BOWL, using an electric mixer at low speed, beat the egg whites and cream of tartar until foamy. Add the salt, increase the mixer speed to medium, and continue beating until soft peaks form. Beat in the vanilla.

GRADUALLY ADD THE GRANULATED SUGAR, 1 tablespoon at a time, beating until meringue forms stiff, glossy peaks.

COMBINE THE CONFECTIONERS' SUGAR, crushed peppermint, walnuts, and chocolate chips in a large bowl. Stir gently to combine. Scoop a large dollop (about 1 cup) of the meringue into the candy mixture to lighten it and gently fold together. Spoon the remaining meringue into the candy/meringue mixture and fold together just until combined, being careful to retain the meringue's stiff peaks.

USE A LARGE SERVING SPOON TO SCOOP TWELVE APPROXIMATELY 1/4-CUP FREE-FORM, cloud-like portions of the meringue onto each of the prepared baking sheets. Reduce the oven temperature to 200°F.

BAKE THE MERINGUES UNTIL VERY CRISP, about 2 hours. Baking the meringues for a long period of time at a very low temperature will ensure that they remain creamy white, and become crisp. If the oven seems too hot or the meringues are beginning to turn color, prop the oven door open slightly with the handle of a wooden spoon. When the meringues are crisp, turn the oven off and let the meringues cool in the oven for 1 to 6 hours. I often make these in the evening, and let the meringues to cool completely in the oven overnight.

STORE THE COOLED MERINGUES IN A TIGHTLY COVERED CONTAINER FOR UP TO 1 WEEK.

Do you fear meringue? Do you wonder why cream of tartar is always added before beating egg whites? Do you break out in a cold sweat wondering if your peaks are soft or stiff? Does the idea of folding anything together fill you with fear? Take heart. These simple steps will have you beating and folding egg whites like a pro in no time, making meringues, chocolate mousse, and angel food cake a snap to prepare.

### SEPARATE COLD EGGS

Egg yolks and whites will separate easily and cleanly when they are very cold. Crack the egg in half over a clean bowl and tip the firm yolk from shell half to shell half, allowing the white to fall into the bowl beneath. If this sounds tricky, simply crack the egg and open into one of your hands, allowing the egg white to dribble through your fingers into the bowl, then closing them to keep the yolk nestled in your hand. For the greatest volume, allow your egg whites to come to room temperature before beating.

### KEEP THE WHITES FAT-FREE

Egg whites must be free of any traces of yolk or other fats to whip up properly. Oil and grease inhibits the egg white's ability to trap and hold air. If you notice a touch of yolk floating in your egg whites, remove it with one of the empty egg shells; the yolk is magically attracted to the shell and will be easier to remove.

### ADD CREAM OF TARTAR

Before the advent of electric mixers, egg whites were beaten in copper bowls with wire whisks. The elements in the copper combined with the egg whites to stabilize them and enhance their ability to foam properly. Adding cream of tartar to the egg whites also ensures that they will develop a dense, creamy foam with maximum volume. A pinch of cream of tartar (an acid) guarantees your beaten whites will be more stable and less likely to collapse.

## EGG WHITES 101

### USE A METAL BOWL

If copper bowls aren't available, use a stainless-steel bowl. Plastic bowls are a poor choice as it is impossible to keep them completely free of all traces of oil and grease. Ceramic or glass bowls are too slippery for the egg whites, making it difficult for them to cling together and form a close, tight structure.

### START SLOWLY

To create a more stable egg white foam with fewer chances of collapsing, start beating the whites at low speed, increasing the speed as the whites lose their viscosity and start to bubble and get foamy. Beginning at a lower speed creates smaller, more stable bubbles in the foam. At this point, add the cream of tartar to stabilize the foam you have started, and a pinch of salt for flavor.

### BEAT TO SOFT PEAKS

Soft peaks are formed when the egg whites develop soft, cloud-like mounds with well-defined peaks that slowly curve down when the beaters are lifted. Softly beaten egg whites will not yet cling to the sides of the bowl, but shift from side to side in one mass when the bowl is tilted. Egg whites beaten to the soft peak stage are the perfect consistency for folding into soufflés, mousses, and cake batters. They are firm enough to hold their shape without deflating, but are easily incorporated into other ingredients. Egg whites beaten to soft peaks will continue to expand in the oven when baked, ensuring high-rising cakes.

### BEAT TO STIFF, GLOSSY PEAKS

Egg whites beaten to stiff, glossy peaks will be snow-white and have a dense, creamy texture with peaks that stand firmly upright when the beaters are lifted. Egg whites beaten to stiff peaks usually have sugar beaten in to them, and are so firm that they will not fall out of the bowl if it were turned upside down. Until you are familiar enough to visually judge the egg whites consistency, feel free to stop the mixer and check how firmly the peaks stand up when the beaters are lifted. Egg whites beaten to stiff peaks hold their shape beautifully, making them perfect for Pavlovas, meringue cookies, and meringue toppings for pies.

### DON'T OVERBEAT

After the egg whites achieve their glossiest, firmest peak, stop beating! Overbeating causes the whites to separate and become dry and granular, which eventually causes them to collapse.

### FOLDING

To fold beaten egg whites into a batter or other ingredients, always add the whites to the batter, never the batter to the whites (which can deflate the meringue, turning it into a watery puddle). Add one-third of the egg whites to the batter first, using a rubber spatula or large balloon whisk to gently fold together, lightening the original batter. Add the rest of the beaten egg whites all at once and carefully fold them in, scooping the batter up from the bottom of the bowl over the egg whites to gently incorporate them together. Continue just until the two mixtures are combined, being careful not to overmix them. It's better to play it safe and avoid overmixing, even if a little streak or two of egg white remains, to avoid deflating the whole mixture.

This may not be the brown sugar that Mick Jagger was singing about, but this gutsy, brown-sugar pound cake, with its moist, tender, slightly chewy crust, is just as delicious. It's packed with so much flavor, it is easy to eat half the cake before you know what you are doing. It's great on its own, but is also delicious as part of the Grilled Chocolate Pound-Cake Sandwiches (page 36). If you are using this pound cake as part of another recipe, eliminate the glaze.

# Ooh! Brown Sugar! and Almond Pound Cake

SERVES 10 TO 12

2 CUPS BLEACHED ALL-PURPOSE FLOUR, SIFTED THEN MEASURED

1 1/4 CUPS GROUND ALMOND MEAL OR ALMOND FLOUR (SEE PAGE 89)

1 TEASPOON BAKING POWDER

1/2 TEASPOON SALT

1 1/2 CUPS (3 STICKS) UNSALTED BUTTER, AT ROOM TEMPERATURE

8 OUNCES CREAM CHEESE, AT ROOM TEMPERATURE

2 CUPS FIRMLY PACKED LIGHT BROWN SUGAR

1 CUP CONFECTIONERS' SUGAR, SIFTED

1 TABLESPOON PURE VANILLA EXTRACT

1 TEASPOON PURE ALMOND EXTRACT

6 LARGE EGGS, AT ROOM TEMPERATURE

**FOR THE BROWN SUGAR GLAZE:**

4 TABLESPOONS BUTTER

1/2 CUP WATER

1 CUP FIRMLY PACKED LIGHT BROWN SUGAR

POSITION A RACK IN THE MIDDLE OF THE OVEN AND PREHEAT TO 325°F. Spray a Bundt pan, 10-inch tube pan, or two 8 1/2-by-4 1/2-inch loaf pans with nonstick cooking spray.

IN A BOWL, sift together the flour, almond meal, baking powder, and salt. Set aside.

IN A LARGE BOWL, using an electric mixer set on medium speed, beat butter and cream cheese together until smooth and creamy. Gradually beat in the brown sugar and confectioner's sugar and continue beating until pale and fluffy. Beat in the vanilla and almond extracts.

ADD THE EGGS TO THE BUTTER MIXTURE ONE AT A TIME, beating well after each addition. Fold the flour and almond mixture into the batter by hand, using a rubber spatula or large balloon whisk, until no traces of flour remain and the batter is smooth.

SPOON THE BATTER INTO PREPARED PAN(S). Bake until a skewer inserted into the center of the cake comes out clean, 75 to 90 minutes.

MEANWHILE, MAKE THE GLAZE: Combine the butter, water, and brown sugar in a saucepan over low heat and cook until sugar and butter are melted. Increase the heat to high and bring to a boil. Boil until the glaze is thick and syrupy, about 5 minutes.

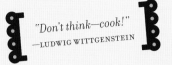

TRANSFER THE CAKE TO A WIRE RACK. Let cool 5 minutes before unmolding onto the rack. Use a wooden skewer to poke holes in the top of the cake and drizzle with the warm glaze. Let the cake cool completely on the wire rack.

AT THIS POINT, the cake can be wrapped well in plastic wrap and stored at room temperature for up to 3 days, or frozen for up to 1 month. If you want to freeze the cake, eliminate the glaze.

## VARIATIONS

TO MAKE A HAZELNUT POUND CAKE: Substitute 1¼ cups ground hazelnut meal or hazelnut flour (see page 89) for the almond flour, and substitute 3 cups granulated sugar for the brown sugar and confectioners' sugar. Omit the glaze.

TO MAKE A CHOCOLATE POUND CAKE: Substitute 2¼ cups bleached all-purpose flour and ¾ cup Dutch-processed cocoa powder (see page 45) for the flour and almond flour mixture. Omit the glaze.

Baking soda and baking powder are both chemical leavening agents used in cake, cookie, and quick-bread baking. What is a leavening agent? A leavening agent is simply something that helps the batter rise. There are many different leavening agents, including yeast, used to help bread rise; steam, which is released when the water in a dough evaporates and is trapped by the crust, making the batter puff up, as in popovers and pâte à choux; and air. Chemical leavening agents like baking soda and baking powder expand the air bubbles already creamed, whipped, beaten, or stirred into a batter. When either baking soda or baking powder is added (or sometimes both), they add volume and texture to the final cake, cookie, or quick bread.

## RISING TO THE OCCASION:
### *When to Use Baking Soda or Baking Powder*

### BAKING SODA

Also known as bicarbonate of soda, baking soda is an alkaline chemical. As a leavening agent, it needs an acidic ingredient in the batter to work properly. Acidic ingredients include natural cocoa powder, buttermilk, yogurt, sour cream, honey, molasses, brown sugar, applesauce, lemon and other citrus juices, and vinegar.

When baking soda is moistened and mixed with an acidic ingredient, it immediately forms carbon dioxide gas, which starts to enlarge the air pockets in the batter. When using baking soda, it is imperative that you move fast and get your batter into the oven as quickly as possible. If the batter stands waiting too long, the leavening power of the baking soda will dissipate and batter will not rise properly. Along with leavening, and balancing the acidity in batters, baking soda also assists in developing the color and texture of baked goods.

### BAKING POWDER

Baking powder is a combination of baking soda (an alkali) and cream of tartar or calcium acid phosphate (an acid). Most baking powder is "double acting," which means it starts creating a small amount of carbon dioxide gas when combined with the wet ingredients in a batter and then goes on to release the lion's share of its carbon dioxide gas when warmed by the heat of the oven. Unlike batters made with baking soda alone, recipes made with baking powder are a little more forgiving, and can wait a little longer before baking (perhaps 15 minutes or so) and still retain all of their leavening ability.

When it comes to baking, especially cake baking, it's important to use the proper amount of baking powder or baking soda in your batter. Too little baking soda will deliver a dry cake, and too little baking powder will yield a tough, heavy cake with poor volume. But according to food scientist and cookbook author Shirley Corriher, cakes that fall more than likely contain too much, rather than too little, leavening. If a cake batter contains too much baking powder, the air bubbles will grow too large and then pop before the cake is completely baked and therefore stable, causing it to fall. She recommends the following guidelines:

- 1 to 1¼ teaspoons baking powder per 1 cup of flour

- ¼ teaspoon baking soda per 1 cup flour (since baking soda is 4 times more powerful than baking powder)

These are very general guidelines, however, as the addition of large quantities of heavy ingredients such as dried fruit, fruit purées, grated carrots (for a carrot cake), or large quantities of liquids or fats may necessitate a slight increase in the leavening needed. When it comes to cookies and brownies, consider the texture desired; the more leavening added, the lighter and cakier the texture will be. For a dense, chewy texture, only a small amount of a leavening agent is needed. For example, only a small amount of baking soda and baking powder are added to chocolate chip cookie dough, which contributes to the cookies' chewy texture and golden brown color.

My parents have a giant fig tree in their backyard. For many years, in late August just as the figs grew fat and started to fall to the ground, my great-grandmother drove up in her old Cadillac carrying her big blue enamel preserving pan to make fig jam. She and my mother gathered and picked every sticky, ripe fig—my great-grandmother's eagle eye letting no ripe fig go ungathered. They made fig jam all day, the air in that kitchen growing hotter, heavier, and sweeter as the jam slowly cooked in the oven. They made fig cakes and homemade fig bars from the jam. I never helped, but tried to escape the heavy, still air to read a book in the hammock under the wisteria that twined around our garage. I still haven't learned how to make jam from fresh figs, which, if you can find it, can be $10 or more for a little 8-ounce jar. Every year I want to make fig jam with my mother, but those hot August days still scare me off. You can make dried fig jam any time of year, and it is almost as good as the jam my mother and great-grandmother made. Use Calimyrna figs for a mild, sweet flavor.

# Fig Cake SERVES 15

**FOR THE DRIED FIG JAM:**

10 OUNCES DRIED CALIMYRNA FIGS

1 CUP SUGAR

3 CUPS WATER

**FOR THE CAKE:**

2 CUPS UNBLEACHED ALL-PURPOSE FLOUR

2 TEASPOONS BAKING SODA

2 TEASPOONS GROUND CINNAMON

1/2 TEASPOON SALT

1/2 CUP VEGETABLE OIL

1/2 CUP (1 STICK) UNSALTED BUTTER, AT ROOM TEMPERATURE

1 CUP SUGAR

2 LARGE EGGS

1 TEASPOON PURE VANILLA EXTRACT

1 CUP BOILING WATER

1 1/2 CUPS CHOPPED WALNUTS, TOASTED (SEE PAGE 89)

CONFECTIONERS' SUGAR FOR SPRINKLING

**TO MAKE THE JAM:** Coarsely chop the figs and combine with the sugar and water in a large, heavy-bottomed saucepan. Bring to a boil over high heat. Reduce the heat to achieve a gentle simmer and cook the figs, covered, until tender, about 1 hour. Let cool slightly, then purée the mixture in a food processor until smooth. You should have about 2 cups.

**POSITION A RACK IN THE MIDDLE OF THE OVEN AND PREHEAT TO 350°F.** Lightly grease a 9-by-13-inch baking pan with oil or lightly spray with nonstick cooking spray.

**TO MAKE THE CAKE:** Sift together the flour, baking soda, cinnamon, and salt into a small bowl. Set aside. In a large bowl, using an electric mixer set at medium speed, beat together the oil, butter, and sugar until creamy and combined. Beat in the eggs, one at a time, beating well after each addition. Beat in the vanilla. Using a rubber spatula, fold in the flour mixture just until combined. Stir in the boiling water, 2 cups of the fig jam (but no more, or the cake will be too soft), and walnuts. Spread the batter evenly in the prepared pan. Bake until a wooden skewer inserted in the center comes out clean, 30 to 35 minutes.

**TRANSFER TO A WIRE RACK AND LET COOL.** Sprinkle cake with confectioners' sugar. Cut into 15 squares and serve.

When we were first married, my husband and I spent a wonderful week on the little island of Kalymnos in Greece, swimming in the ocean, tanning to an unhealthy mahogany color, and lunching in little beachside cafes (usually surrounded by an inordinate number of overly friendly cats). It was wonderful, but of course, my favorite part of the trip was discovering all the delicious desserts. I love this light cake because it reminds me of my favorite Greek desserts, sticky with syrup and thick with nuts. It's best made early in the day, or even the day before you plan to serve it, to give the cake time to soak up all the delicious, sweet syrup.

# Walnut Torte with Dark Rum Syrup

SERVES 10

3 CUPS VERY FINELY CHOPPED WALNUTS, TOASTED (SEE PAGE 89)

1/2 CUP UNBLEACHED ALL-PURPOSE FLOUR

1 TEASPOON BAKING POWDER

PINCH OF SALT

6 LARGE EGGS, SEPARATED, AND AT ROOM TEMPERATURE

1 1/2 CUPS SUGAR

1 TEASPOON PURE VANILLA EXTRACT

PINCH OF CREAM OF TARTAR

**FOR THE RUM SYRUP:**

1 3/4 CUPS WATER

2 CUPS SUGAR

2 OR 3 TABLESPOONS DARK RUM

POSITION A RACK IN THE MIDDLE OF THE OVEN AND PREHEAT TO 350°F.

IN A LARGE BOWL, stir together the walnuts, flour, baking powder, and salt.

PLACE THE EGG YOLKS IN A BOWL AND THE WHITES IN A LARGE STAINLESS-STEEL MIXING BOWL. Whisk the egg yolks, gradually adding 1/2 cup of the sugar a little at a time. Keep whisking until the sugar is incorporated, the yolks are thick and creamy, and the sugar is dissolved and not gritty. Whisk in the vanilla. Fold the walnut mixture into the beaten egg yolks. The mixture will be very thick. Set aside.

USING AN ELECTRIC MIXER SET AT LOW SPEED, beat the egg whites and cream of tartar together until frothy. Increase the mixer speed to medium and beat the egg whites until soft peaks form. Increase the mixer speed to high and add the remaining 1 cup sugar to the egg whites, 1 tablespoon at a time. Beat just until all the sugar is incorporated and the whites form stiff, glossy peaks.

ADD A LARGE DOLLOP OF THE EGG WHITES TO THE WALNUT MIXTURE AND FOLD IN TO LOOSEN AND LIGHTEN THE BATTER. Carefully fold the remaining egg whites into the batter, taking care not to deflate them. Fold just until the egg whites are fully incorporated into the walnut batter and only a trace of white streaks remain.

LIGHTLY GREASE A 10-INCH ROUND SPRINGFORM PAN OR SPRAY LIGHTLY WITH NONSTICK COOKING SPRAY. Spoon the batter into the pan and smooth the top with the back of a spatula. Bake until a wooden skewer inserted into the center of the torte comes out clean, 45 to 50 minutes.

CONTINUED

110

CONTINUED

**WHILE THE TORTE IS BAKING, MAKE THE SYRUP:** Combine the water and sugar in a saucepan over medium heat and cook until the sugar dissolves. Increase the heat to high and bring to a rolling boil. Reduce the heat to medium-low and simmer until the mixture is the consistency of thick maple syrup, about 10 minutes. Remove from the heat and stir in the rum. Let the syrup cool slightly until it is just warm.

**TRANSFER THE TORTE TO A WIRE RACK.** Pierce the torte in the pan all over with a wooden skewer and slowly pour the warm syrup over the torte while it, too, is still warm. Let the torte cool completely while the syrup soaks all the way through it. When the cake is completely cool, it can be covered with plastic wrap while still in the pan and chilled until ready to serve. If you like, it can also be served at room temperature. To remove the torte from the pan, run a thin spatula or knife around the edge of the torte to loosen it before removing the sides of the pan. Leave the torte on the base of the springform pan, as it will be too delicate and syrupy to successfully transfer it to another plate without tearing.

**SERVE WEDGES OF THIS DELICIOUS TORTE AS THE GREEKS DO,** with little cups of thick, black coffee or a nescafé, made by muddling a scoop of instant coffee with sugar and a splash of milk in the bottom of a tall glass. Top the coffee with ice water and stir to a froth.

It may be called devil's food, but this cake is pure heaven for the chocoholics among you. Devil's food is distinguished by its heavy jolt of chocolate flavor, often, as it is here, a combination of cocoa powder and melted dark chocolate. Dark brown sugar and either sour cream or buttermilk are usually in the mix as well, making for a dense, rich, old-fashioned layer cake perfect with the Chocolate Mousse Buttercreammm. I made this cake for my father's sixty-fifth birthday; it is the perfect, full-bodied, festive dessert for all occasions as auspicious as that one.

# Devil's Food Cake SERVES 8 TO 10
## with Chocolate Mousse Buttercreammm

1/3 CUP DUTCH-PROCESSED COCOA POWDER (SEE PAGE 45), SIFTED

1 TEASPOON INSTANT ESPRESSO POWDER

4 OUNCES SEMISWEET OR BITTER-SWEET CHOCOLATE, FINELY CHOPPED

1 CUP BOILING WATER

2 TEASPOONS PURE VANILLA EXTRACT

1 CUP BUTTERMILK

1/2 CUP (1 STICK) UNSALTED BUTTER, AT ROOM TEMPERATURE

1/2 CUP VEGETABLE OIL

1 CUP FIRMLY PACKED DARK BROWN SUGAR

1 CUP GRANULATED SUGAR

3 LARGE EGGS, AT ROOM TEMPERATURE

2 1/4 CUPS CAKE FLOUR

1 TEASPOON BAKING SODA

1/2 TEASPOON SALT

CHOCOLATE MOUSSE BUTTERCREAMMM (PAGE 112)

POSITION A RACK IN THE MIDDLE OF THE OVEN AND PREHEAT TO 350°F. Lightly grease two 9-inch round cake pans or spray with nonstick cooking spray. Line the bottoms of the pans with circles of parchment or waxed paper. Grease the paper or spray lightly with cooking spray.

IN A LARGE BOWL, combine the cocoa powder, espresso powder, and chocolate. Pour in the boiling water and stir until the chocolate is melted and the mixture is smooth. Stir in the vanilla. Let the mixture cool, then stir in the buttermilk.

IN ANOTHER BOWL, using an electric mixer set at medium speed, beat the butter and oil together until light and fluffy. Add the sugars and beat until creamy. Beat in the eggs, one at a time, beating well after each addition.

SIFT TOGETHER THE FLOUR, baking soda, and salt onto a sheet of waxed paper. Add one-third of the flour mixture to the batter and beat at low speed for a few seconds, just until combined. Beat in half of the chocolate-buttermilk mixture, again beating just for a few seconds until combined. Scrape down the sides of the bowl with a rubber spatula. Beat in another one-third of the remaining flour mixture for no more than a few seconds, just until combined. Add the remaining chocolate-buttermilk mixture, beating just for a few seconds until combined. Finally, fold in the remaining one-third of the flour mixture by hand, using a large balloon whisk or rubber spatula, just until no streaks of flour remain.

DIVIDE THE BATTER BETWEEN THE PREPARED CAKE PANS AND SPREAD EVENLY. Bake until a wooden skewer inserted in the center of a cake comes out clean, 25 to 30 minutes. Transfer to wire racks and let cool for 5 to 10 minutes. Invert the cakes onto the racks and peel the parchment paper from the layers. Let cool completely before frosting.

CONTINUED

CONTINUED

HALVE EACH CAKE LAYER HORIZONTALLY USING A LONG SERRATED KNIFE, for a total of 4 thin cake layers. Place one layer cut-side up on a serving plate and top with 1 cup of the Chocolate Mousse Buttercreammm, spreading it evenly. Continue stacking the cake, spreading 1 cup buttercream in between each layer and placing the top layer cut-side down. Frost the top and sides of the cake with the remaining buttercream, giving the top a few decorative swirls. Cut into wedges and serve.

## Chocolate Mousse Buttercreammm MAKES ABOUT 5 CUPS

or enough to generously frost one 9-inch layer cake or 24 cupcakes

**This classic buttercream has the deep, rich chocolate flavor and creamy texture of the perfect chocolate mousse.**

112

6 LARGE EGGS

1 1/2 CUPS SUGAR

2 TABLESPOONS DUTCH-PROCESSED COCOA POWDER (SEE PAGE 45)

1 TEASPOON PURE VANILLA EXTRACT

PINCH OF SALT

1 1/2 POUNDS (6 STICKS) COLD UNSALTED BUTTER

8 TO 12 OUNCES SEMISWEET CHOCOLATE, MELTED (SEE PAGE 20)

WHISK TOGETHER THE EGGS, sugar, and cocoa powder in the metal bowl of a stand mixer.

FILL A LARGE SAUTÉ PAN OR SKILLET WITH WATER AND BRING TO A SIMMER OVER MEDIUM-HIGH HEAT. Place the mixing bowl in the simmering water and whisk the egg mixture constantly until the sugar is completely dissolved and the mixture is thick and fluffy and very hot, 3 to 4 minutes. Use an instant-read thermometer to check the temperature of the mixture; it should be anywhere between 120° and 140°F.

REMOVE THE BOWL FROM THE SIMMERING WATER AND, using the whisk attachment, beat the eggs at medium-high speed until they are tripled in volume and form soft peaks and the bottom of the bowl is completely cool to the touch, about 10 minutes. Beat in the vanilla and salt.

WHILE THE EGGS ARE MIXING, unwrap the individual sticks and rewrap them loosely in plastic wrap. Pound the butter 5 or 6 times with a rolling pin, or until the butter is soft and malleable but still cool.

WITH THE MIXER SPEED STILL ON MEDIUM HIGH, add the butter, approximately 2 tablespoons at a time, to the egg mixture, beating in each addition until it is incorporated. Don't start to panic if the buttercream seems too liquidy or looks curdled as you beat in the butter. It will magically emulsify into a smooth, creamy frosting by the time the last bit of butter is mixed in. Hold your breath and keep going.

WHEN THE BUTTERCREAM IS SMOOTH AND GLOSSY WITH A SUBTLE BROWN TINT FROM THE COCOA POWDER, turn off the mixer and, using a rubber spatula, carefully fold in about two-thirds of the melted chocolate. Taste the buttercream. You can add as much of the remaining melted chocolate as you like for an even richer, denser buttercream.

The importance of using the right type of flour when baking cannot be overemphasized. In the world of white wheat flour, all-purpose is not the only way to go. Cakes need a different flour than do cream puffs, cookies, and quick breads; and pie crust needs a different flour than a loaf of sourdough bread will. The following list of flours and their uses will help make your baking a breeze, and ensure delicious results every time.

### BREAD FLOUR

Bread flour is made from hard wheat with a high protein content—12 to 14 percent. High-protein flours contain large amounts of gluten, which works well with slow-growing yeasts to develop springy, chewy breads that hold their shape.

## THE SCOOP ON FLOUR

### UNBLEACHED ALL-PURPOSE FLOUR

All-purpose flour is made from a mixture of hard and soft wheat, and contains 10 to 12 percent protein. Unbleached all-purpose flour is strong enough for pâte à choux, popovers, puff pastry, and some sturdier cookies.

### BLEACHED ALL-PURPOSE FLOUR

Bleached all-purpose flour has slightly less protein than unbleached all-purpose flour, making it a touch softer, so it is a better choice for sturdy cakes, cookies, pie crusts, quick breads, and biscuits. Southern brands of all-purpose flour (very popular with Southern cooks, especially for making biscuits) are made from soft wheat—"soft" meaning they contain less protein than unbleached all-purpose flours milled in the northern states (which includes many well-known national brands of all-purpose flour). Use soft, Southern-wheat, all-purpose flour only when called for, or in recipes calling for bleached all-purpose flour.

### CAKE FLOUR

Soft, fine-textured cake flour has the lowest protein content of all the white wheat flours, 6 to 8 percent. This bleached flour has a low gluten content and a smooth, velvety, almost creamy texture. It is an excellent choice for delicate, fine-textured cakes. If you don't have cake flour, you can make your own version by substituting 1 cup cake flour with ¾ cup bleached all-purpose flour mixed with 2 tablespoons cornstarch.

### SELF-RISING FLOUR

Self-rising flour contains salt and baking powder. Do not use self-rising flour unless the recipe specifically calls for it; otherwise you run the risk of adding too much salt and leavening agents to your recipe.

### HOW TO MEASURE FLOUR

Use the classic "spoon and sweep" method for measuring flour accurately.

· While in the bag or storage container, stir the flour with a wooden spoon to aerate it slightly, but do not sift it.

· Spoon the flour into the measuring cup without shaking or leveling it, until the flour mounds over the top of the cup.

· Use the back of a knife to level the top of the cup, brushing any excess flour back into the bag or storage container.

Visions of umbrella drinks and Caribbean pirates may dance through your head when you take your first bite of this rich, pecan-encrusted cake. It is really a cross between a rum cake and a pound cake, and marries the best of both traditions in one moist, banana-flecked, rum-drenched dream. Banana cake in all its many incarnations is pretty hard to resist, but I think this one is sublime. It is dense, without being heavy, and the spicy molasses kick from the dark rum doesn't overwhelm the deep banana flavor—it only enhances it.

# Bahama Mama Banana Rum Cake

SERVES 10

**FOR THE DARK RUM GLAZE:**

1/2 CUP (1 STICK) UNSALTED BUTTER

1/4 CUP WATER

1/2 CUP FIRMLY PACKED LIGHT OR DARK BROWN SUGAR

1/2 CUP GRANULATED SUGAR

1/2 CUP DARK RUM

**FOR THE CAKE:**

1 1/2 CUPS CHOPPED PECANS, TOASTED (SEE PAGE 89)

1 1/2 CUPS (3 STICKS) UNSALTED BUTTER

2 CUPS GRANULATED SUGAR

1 CUP FIRMLY PACKED LIGHT OR DARK BROWN SUGAR

5 LARGE EGGS, AT ROOM TEMPERATURE

1 CUP MASHED VERY RIPE BANANAS (ABOUT 3 MEDIUM BANANAS)

2 TEASPOONS PURE VANILLA EXTRACT

3 TABLESPOONS DARK RUM

3 CUPS BLEACHED ALL-PURPOSE FLOUR

1 TEASPOON BAKING SODA

1 TEASPOON BAKING POWDER

1 TEASPOON SALT

3/4 CUP SOUR CREAM

TO MAKE THE GLAZE: Combine the butter, water, and sugars in a heavy-bottomed saucepan over medium-high heat and bring to a boil. Immediately reduce the heat to medium-low and simmer for 5 minutes. Remove from the heat and stir in the rum. Set aside and keep warm.

TO MAKE THE CAKE: Position a rack in the middle of the oven and preheat to 350°F. Spray a 10-cup tube pan with nonstick cooking spray. Sprinkle the pecans in the bottom of the pan. Set aside.

IN A LARGE BOWL, with an electric mixer set on medium speed, beat together the butter and sugars until the mixture is light and fluffy. Beat in the eggs, one at a time, mixing well after each addition. Beat in the mashed bananas, vanilla, and rum. Sift the flour, baking soda, baking powder, and salt over the batter and fold in using a rubber spatula, just until no streaks of flour remain. Fold in the sour cream. Spoon the batter over the nuts in the pan and spread to the edge of the pan using the back of the rubber spatula.

BAKE UNTIL A WOODEN SKEWER INSERTED IN THE CENTER OF THE CAKE COMES OUT WITH NO MORE THAN A FEW MOIST CRUMBS CLINGING TO IT, 60 to 80 minutes. Transfer to a wire rack and let cool for 5 minutes. Use a wooden skewer to poke holes all over the cake and pour 1/4 cup of the warm glaze over the cake. Let the cake cool for 5 minutes more. Place a serving platter over the pan and invert to release the cake onto the platter. Spoon the remaining glaze over the cake, a little at a time, and let stand until the glaze is completely absorbed into the cake. If the glaze starts to pool at the base of the cake, use a small metal spatula to spread it up and around the sides of the cake. As the glaze hardens, this will encase the cake in a rummy, sugary shell.

LET THE CAKE COOL COMPLETELY BEFORE CUTTING INTO WEDGES AND SERVING. This cake will last 2 to 3 days if covered well.

There is no doubt that chemistry and baking are sisters. Otherwise how to explain the transformation of butter, with the simple application of heat, into the nutty, toasty elixir known in French as *beurre noisette*? This delicious browned butter has an aromatic and slightly sweet caramelized flavor that accentuates the flavor of the almonds in this cake and contributes to its deep, rich flavor. The addition of caramel apples makes this the perfect autumnal dessert, but fresh berries and whipped cream would make an equally tasty combination in the spring or summer.

# Brown-Butter Almond Cake with Caramel Apples SERVES 8

1 CUP (2 STICKS) UNSALTED BUTTER

1 3/4 CUPS BLEACHED ALL-PURPOSE FLOUR

1 3/4 TEASPOONS BAKING POWDER

1/2 TEASPOON SALT

1/2 CUP SLICED ALMONDS, FINELY GROUND (SEE PAGE 89)

1 ROLL (7 OUNCES) ALMOND PASTE

1 CUP SUGAR

1 TEASPOON PURE VANILLA EXTRACT

3 LARGE EGGS

2 LARGE EGG YOLKS

**FOR THE CARAMEL APPLES:**

4 TABLESPOONS UNSALTED BUTTER

1/3 CUP FIRMLY PACKED LIGHT BROWN SUGAR

1/3 CUP GRANULATED SUGAR

1/2 TEASPOON PURE VANILLA EXTRACT

PINCH OF SALT

4 GRANNY SMITH APPLES, PEELED, CORED AND CUT INTO 1/2-INCH SLICES

CONFECTIONERS' SUGAR FOR DUSTING

SWEETENED WHIPPED CREAM (PAGE 43) OR VANILLA, CARAMEL, OR COFFEE ICE CREAM FOR SERVING

POSITION A RACK IN THE MIDDLE OF THE OVEN AND PREHEAT TO 400°F. Grease a 9-inch round cake pan or spray with nonstick cooking spray. Line the bottom of the pan with a circle of parchment paper.

MELT THE BUTTER IN A SAUCEPAN OVER LOW HEAT. When melted, increase the heat to high and bring the butter to a boil. Continue cooking the butter until the solids at the bottom of the pan begin to brown. As the solids begin to caramelize, the butter will develop a sweet, nutty aroma—this should take about 5 minutes. Immediately remove the pan from the heat and strain the butter through a fine-mesh sieve into a heatproof bowl (this will prevent the butter from cooking any longer and possibly burning). Let the butter cool completely.

IN ANOTHER BOWL, sift together the flour, baking powder, and salt. Stir in the ground almonds and set aside.

BREAK THE ALMOND PASTE INTO SMALL PIECES AND COMBINE IN A BOWL WITH THE SUGAR. Using an electric mixer set on low speed, beat until the almond paste and sugar are combined, with a fine, sandy texture. If the almond paste is too hard, micro-wave on medium for 30 to 40 seconds to soften. Beat in the vanilla. Beat the whole eggs and egg yolks into the mixture, one at a time, beating well after each addition. Use a rubber spatula to carefully fold the flour mixture into the batter, just until incorporated. Finally, fold the cooled browned butter into the batter.

CONTINUED

CONTINUED

**SPOON THE BATTER INTO THE PREPARED PAN AND SPREAD EVENLY.** Bake for 10 minutes. Reduce the oven temperature to 350°F and continue baking until a wooden skewer inserted into the center of the cake comes out clean, 30 to 35 minutes.

**MEANWHILE, MAKE THE APPLES:** Melt the butter in a 12-inch sauté pan or skillet over medium heat. Add the sugars and stir until they dissolve into the butter and the mixture is golden brown and bubbling. Stir in the vanilla and salt. Add the apples to the mixture and simmer, uncovered, stirring frequently. Cook until the apples are tender and caramelized, 15 to 20 minutes.

**TRANSFER THE CAKE TO A WIRE RACK AND LET COOL FOR 10 MINUTES.** Invert the cake onto a serving platter and peel away the parchment paper. Dust with confectioners' sugar and cut into wedges. Serve with the warm caramel apples and a dollop of whipped cream or a scoop of ice cream.

Grade B maple syrup is thicker, less refined, and stronger in flavor than the traditional grade A syrup that is usually reserved for pancakes (I like grade B better on pancakes, too). This is a rich, full-bodied, sticky nut pie. Although it is a delicious stand-in for the more popular pecan pie, it really deserves a place of honor at the table all by itself.

# Maple Walnut Pie SERVES 6 TO 8

3 LARGE EGGS, LIGHTLY BEATEN

1 CUP GRADE B MAPLE SYRUP

1/2 CUP FIRMLY PACKED LIGHT BROWN SUGAR

1 TEASPOON PURE VANILLA EXTRACT

1/4 TEASPOON SALT

3 TABLESPOONS UNSALTED BUTTER, MELTED AND COOLED

2 CUPS CHOPPED WALNUTS, TOASTED (SEE PAGE 89)

ONE 9-INCH PIE SHELL, UNBAKED

POSITION A RACK IN THE MIDDLE OF THE OVEN AND PREHEAT TO 450°F.

IN A BOWL, beat together the eggs, maple syrup, brown sugar, vanilla, and salt until smooth. Beat in the cooled melted butter and the walnuts.

POUR THE FILLING INTO THE PIE SHELL AND BAKE FOR 10 MINUTES. Reduce the oven temperature to 350°F and bake until the pie crust is golden and flaky and the filling is set, 30 to 35 minutes longer. Let cool on a wire rack to room temperature before serving.

If you are going to the trouble of making pie, why make only one when it's just as easy to make two? I love apple crumble pie, and the more sweet, buttery crumble, the better. A mixture of Granny Smith and Golden Delicious apples makes a delicious bubbling filling with just the right tasty combination of tart and tender. I think clear glass pie pans are better than metal or ceramic pans—the crust seems to stay crisper, and it is much easier to gauge how well it is browning just by looking, so no guesswork is needed.

# Double-Crumble Hot Apple Pies

MAKES TWO 9-INCH PIES; SERVES 12 TO 16

1 RECIPE PERFECT PIE CRUST (PAGE 126)

**FOR THE CRUMBLE:**

2 CUPS BLEACHED ALL-PURPOSE FLOUR

1½ CUPS OLD-FASHIONED ROLLED OATS

2½ CUPS FIRMLY PACKED LIGHT BROWN SUGAR

½ TEASPOON GROUND CINNAMON

⅛ TEASPOON FRESHLY GRATED NUTMEG

¼ TEASPOON SALT

1½ CUPS (3 STICKS) UNSALTED BUTTER, MELTED

**FOR THE APPLE FILLING:**

6 MEDIUM GRANNY SMITH APPLES, PEELED, CORED, AND SLICED ¼-INCH THICK

6 MEDIUM GOLDEN DELICIOUS APPLES, PEELED, CORED, AND SLICED ¼-INCH THICK

JUICE OF ½ A LEMON

¼ CUP ALL-PURPOSE FLOUR

½ CUP SUGAR

⅛ TEASPOON FRESHLY GROUND NUTMEG

¼ TEASPOON SALT

PREHEAT THE OVEN TO 400°F.

ROLL OUT EACH ROUND OF PIE DOUGH INTO A 12-INCH CIRCLE. Gently fit each round in a 9-inch glass pie pan, allowing the excess dough to hang over the edge of the pie pan. Set aside.

TO MAKE THE CRUMBLE: Combine the flour, oats, brown sugar, cinnamon, nutmeg, and salt in a bowl. Add the melted butter and stir together until the dry mixture is moistened with the melted butter and is crumbly. Refrigerate until needed.

TO MAKE THE FILLING: In a very large bowl, toss together the sliced apples with the lemon juice, flour, sugar, nutmeg, and salt. Divide the apples between the dough-lined pie pans. Trim the edges of the dough and fold them under and crimp with your fingers to make a decorative border.

DIVIDE THE CRUMBLE BETWEEN THE TWO PIES AND SPREAD EVENLY OVER THE APPLES. You should have a generous amount of crumble for each pie.

BAKE UNTIL THE CRUST AND CRUMBLE ARE GOLDEN BROWN AND THE APPLES ARE TENDER AND BUBBLING, 60 to 75 minutes. Let cool on a wire rack for 20 to 30 minutes before serving.

*I love the buttery, sweet flavor of macadamias as they rise, floating and bumping together, on top of this rich, chewy, butterscotch filling. This is a wonderful pie to serve in lieu of pecan, alongside a traditional pumpkin, for your Thanksgiving feast.*

# Butterscotch-Bourbon Macadamia Nut Pie SERVES 6 TO 8

1 CUP FIRMLY PACKED LIGHT BROWN SUGAR

¼ CUP PLUS 2 TABLESPOONS ALL-PURPOSE FLOUR

½ TEASPOON SALT

½ CUP (1 STICK) UNSALTED BUTTER, MELTED AND COOLED

2 LARGE EGGS

2 TEASPOONS PURE VANILLA EXTRACT

2 TABLESPOONS BOURBON OR TENNESSEE WHISKEY (SEE PAGE 53)

2 CUPS ROASTED MACADAMIA NUTS, TOASTED (SEE PAGE 89)

ONE 9-INCH PIE SHELL, UNBAKED

POSITION A RACK IN THE MIDDLE OF THE OVEN AND PREHEAT TO 350°F.

IN A LARGE BOWL, stir together the brown sugar, flour, and salt. Stir in the melted butter, eggs, vanilla, and bourbon. Mix well. Coarsely chop 1 cup of the macadamia nuts. Fold in the chopped and whole nuts into the batter and pour into the prepared pie shell.

BAKE UNTIL THE CRUST IS GOLDEN AND FILLING IS SET, 50 to 60 minutes. Let cool completely on a wire rack before serving.

This gooey pie, named for a play on the words *banana* and *toffee*, was invented in 1972 for the dessert menu at an English pub called the Hungry Monk. It has been a popular "pudding" on English menus ever since. The heart of the pie—a chewy, fudgy, toffee filling made from sweetened condensed milk—is very similar to the South American favorite *dulce de leche*. To make ahead of time, prepare the toffee filling and pour into the crust, cover, and refrigerate up to 1 day in advance. Before serving, top the pie with fresh banana slices and mound with whipped cream. Crumbly whole meal English digestive biscuits make the best crust, but graham crackers work well, too.

# Banoffee Pie SERVES 6 TO 8

**FOR THE FILLING:**

2 CANS (14 OUNCES EACH) SWEETENED CONDENSED MILK

1 TEASPOON PURE VANILLA EXTRACT

1/4 CUP FIRMLY PACKED DARK BROWN SUGAR

4 TABLESPOONS UNSALTED BUTTER, MELTED

1/4 TEASPOON SALT

BOILING WATER AS NEEDED

**FOR THE CRUMB CRUST:**

2 1/2 CUPS WHOLEMEAL DIGESTIVE BISCUIT CRUMBS OR GRAHAM CRACKER CRUMBS

1/4 CUP GRANULATED SUGAR

1/2 CUP (1 STICK ) UNSALTED BUTTER, MELTED

**FOR THE TOPPING:**

3 MEDIUM BARELY RIPE BANANAS

2 CUPS HEAVY CREAM

1/3 CUP CONFECTIONERS' SUGAR

1/4 TEASPOON INSTANT ESPRESSO DISSOLVED IN 1 TEASPOON PURE VANILLA EXTRACT

POSITION A RACK IN THE MIDDLE OF THE OVEN AND PREHEAT TO 400°F.

TO MAKE THE FILLING: Stir together the sweetened condensed milk, vanilla, brown sugar, melted butter, and salt. Pour into a 6-cup ovenproof dish and cover with aluminum foil. Place the dish in a 9-by-13-inch baking pan and fill the pan with boiling water until it reaches halfway up the sides of the dish. Bake the milk mixture, stirring every 15 minutes, until it has reduced and thickened and turned a toasty caramel color, 1 1/2 to 2 hours. Remove the pan from the oven and from the water bath and let cool. Reduce the oven temperature to 350°F.

WHILE THE FILLING IS COOLING, PREPARE THE CRUMB CRUST: In a small bowl, combine the biscuit crumbs with the granulated sugar and melted butter. Stir together until the crumbs are completely moistened with the butter. Press them into a 9-inch tart pan 3 inches deep with a removable bottom or a 9-inch pie pan. Bake just until the crumbs become crisp and start to turn a deeper, golden brown, 5 to 7 minutes. Transfer to a wire rack and let cool.

WHEN THE TOFFEE FILLING HAS COOLED SLIGHTLY BUT IS STILL SOFT, spoon it into the cooled crumb crust, spreading it into an even layer. Refrigerate the pie until the filling is set. You can cover the pie with plastic wrap and keep it chilled at this point for up to 24 hours.

TO MAKE THE TOPPING: Peel and slice the bananas into 1/2-inch-thick slices and arrange them over the toffee. In a bowl, using an electric mixer set at medium speed, whip the cream with the confectioners' sugar and espresso mixture until stiff peaks form. Pile the whipped cream on top of the bananas, spreading it toward the edges of the crust (make sure the bananas are completely covered to inhibit their browning). Refrigerate the pie until ready to serve.

My friend Debby Jo Jones taught me how to make Angel Pie at Mountain Meadow Ranch, the one summer we were there together. She was the dinner cook, and cool as a cucumber, even under pressure. Her food was delicious, from her corn fritters to this chewy, nutty, chocolate-studded meringue dessert filled with whipped cream and strawberries.

# Not-So-Angelic Angel Pie SERVES 8

CORNSTARCH FOR SPRINKLING

**FOR THE PIE SHELL:**

3/4 CUP GRAHAM CRACKER CRUMBS

1 CUP FINELY CHOPPED WALNUTS OR PECANS, TOASTED (SEE PAGE 89)

5 OUNCES SEMISWEET CHOCOLATE, VERY FINELY CHOPPED

6 LARGE EGG WHITES, AT ROOM TEMPERATURE

1/2 TEASPOON CREAM OF TARTAR

1/8 TEASPOON SALT

2 CUPS GRANULATED SUGAR

1 TEASPOON PURE VANILLA EXTRACT

**FOR THE FILLING:**

2 CUPS HEAVY CREAM, CHILLED

2/3 CUP CONFECTIONERS' SUGAR, SIFTED

1 TEASPOON PURE VANILLA EXTRACT

3 CUPS FRESH STRAWBERRIES, HULLED AND HALVED, OR FRESH RASPBERRIES

LINE A LARGE BAKING SHEET (NOT AN AIR-CUSHIONED ONE) WITH PARCHMENT PAPER AND SPRINKLE LIGHTLY WITH CORNSTARCH. Set aside. Preheat the oven to 350°F.

TO MAKE THE PIE SHELL: In a large bowl, stir together the graham cracker crumbs, nuts, and chocolate until completely combined. Set aside.

IN ANOTHER BOWL, using an electric mixer set at low speed, beat the egg whites and cream of tartar until foamy. Add the salt, increase the speed to medium-high, and continue beating until soft peaks form. Continue beating, adding the sugar to the egg whites 1 tablespoon at a time until stiff, glossy peaks form. Beat in the vanilla.

FOLD A LARGE DOLLOP OF THE EGG WHITES INTO THE CRUMB MIXTURE TO LIGHTEN IT. Gently fold the remaining egg whites into the crumb mixture just until combined, being careful not to deflate them. Do not overmix.

SPOON THE ENTIRE MIXTURE ONTO THE BAKING SHEET AND, using a metal spatula, quickly spread into an 8- to 10-inch round. Bake until the pie is puffy and golden with a crisp outer shell, 25 to 30 minutes. Transfer to a wire rack and let cool completely.

TO MAKE THE FILLING: Combine the chilled cream, 1/3 cup of the confectioners' sugar, and the vanilla in a bowl. Using an electric mixer set at medium speed, beat until the cream holds firm peaks.

WHEN READY TO SERVE, carefully peel the pie shell from the parchment and place on a serving plate. Fill the center of the shell with the whipped cream. Mix the strawberries with the remaining 1/3 cup confectioners' sugar and pile on top of the cream. Cut into wedges and serve immediately.

Coconut oil may sound like an unusual ingredient for pastry dough, but since it is a solid fat at room temperature it is perfect for baking and has many of the same benefits, without many of the disadvantages, of lard and vegetable shortening. Lard makes the flakiest, most delicious pastry, but many people, I know, are disinclined to use it. Because it has fallen out of favor, it is also hard to find lard that is fresh. Flavorless coconut oil is neither an animal fat like lard nor hydrogenated like vegetable shortening. There have even been studies showing that ingesting the fats found in coconut oil can raise resting metabolism by 50 percent. Let's have another piece of pie!

# Perfect Pie Crust

MAKES ENOUGH PASTRY FOR ONE DOUBLE-CRUST OR TWO SINGLE-CRUST 8- OR 9-INCH PIES

3 CUPS UNBLEACHED ALL-PURPOSE FLOUR

2 TEASPOONS SUGAR

1¼ TEASPOONS SALT

1 CUP (2 STICKS) COLD UNSALTED BUTTER, EACH STICK CUT INTO 16 SMALL PIECES AND FROZEN

6 TABLESPOONS SOLID COCONUT OIL, CUT INTO SMALL BITS AND CHILLED

6 TO 8 TABLESPOONS ICE WATER

2 TEASPOONS FRESH LEMON JUICE

1 LARGE EGG YOLK, BEATEN

SIFT THE FLOUR, sugar, and salt together twice into a large metal mixing bowl. Cut the frozen butter and chilled coconut oil into the flour until it resembles coarse meal combined with little pea-sized bits of flour-dusted butter. (Or, for the same texture, use small pulses to combine the sifted flour and fats together in a food processor fitted with a metal blade.)

WHISK TOGETHER 6 TABLESPOONS OF THE ICE WATER, the lemon juice, and the beaten egg yolk. Dribble the liquid into the flour mixture and stir together with a fork, using a light touch so as not to blend the larger bits of fat into the flour. Stir with the fork just until the dough comes together into a moist, but not sticky, ball. Use your hands to gently gather the dough into a ball. You should still see some tiny pieces of butter in the dough (when the crust bakes, these will melt and create wonderfully flaky layers in the pastry).

DIVIDE THE DOUGH IN TWO AND FLATTEN EACH BALL INTO A ROUND DISK. Wrap in plastic wrap. Refrigerate the dough for at least 30 minutes, or up to overnight. The chilled, well-wrapped dough can also be stored in self-sealing plastic bags and frozen for up to 1 month for later use.

### FLOUR

Use unbleached all-purpose flour for a crust that is strong enough to hold its shape, but will still deliver a crust that is flaky and tender. For extra-light pastry, make sure you measure your flour accurately and then sift it two or three times with the salt to lighten and aerate it.

### FAT

Use a mixture of fats: for example, a combination of butter for flavor, and lard, shortening, or firm coconut oil (see headnote on facing page) for a flaky texture.

### KEEP IT COLD

Dice up the cold butter and shortening and then freeze the smaller pieces before starting your pie dough. The pieces of fat will be small enough to cut into the flour easily, but freezing it guarantees the fat won't start melting before you have finished the dough.

### KEEP IT REALLY COLD

Along with cold fat, you want to use ice water, not just cold water, in your dough.

### CUT IN THE FAT

Cut the frozen fats into the well-sifted flour by hand, using a sharp, heavy-duty pastry blender, or in a food processor fitted with a metal blade. If you cut the fat in by hand it is easier to see the process of turning two separate ingredients into a mixture that looks like a combination of coarse meal mixed in with tiny pea-size bits of butter. If you use a food processor to cut the fat into the flour, use small pulses to control how much of the fat is being cut into the flour, so it still results in small bits of fat among the overall crumbly texture (these little "pea-size" bits of fat are imperative; as they melt, the dough steams apart, causing many thin, flaky layers of pastry to form).

### EGG YOLK AND ACID FOR ADDED TENDERNESS

Acids such as cider vinegar or fresh lemon juice inhibit gluten from forming as you handle the dough, ensuring that the pastry stays delicate and tender and doesn't shrink when it is baked. Whole eggs, or egg yolks alone, also inhibit gluten from forming, as well as adding richness to the pastry and helping it brown.

### CHILL THE DOUGH

Refrigerate the pie dough for at least 30 minutes. This allows the gluten to relax, ensures that the fats are cold and firm, and guarantees that the moisture from the egg and ice water permeates the dough. Make sure the dough is well wrapped in plastic wrap so it doesn't dry out.

### ROLLING OUT THE DOUGH

Use a rolling pin lightly dusted with flour, and roll the dough onto a sheet of parchment paper that is also lightly dusted with flour. Rolling the dough on parchment prevents it from sticking to the countertop, as well as preventing the use of too much flour (which can toughen the dough). As you roll out the dough you will notice tiny little dots of cold butter, which is a good thing! These will ensure a light, flaky crust.

## TIPS FOR THE PERFECT PIE CRUST

### USE A GLASS PIE PAN

I like to use a glass pie pan over a metal or ceramic pan. Inexpensive tempered glass pie pans like Pyrex allow the pie dough to brown evenly, with the added plus of being able to visually check the color of the crust as it bakes.

4

# DO TRY THIS AT HOME!

*Over-The-Top Treats for
the Kid in All of Us*

The word "artisanal" is
probably not going to pop up in this
chapter. Neither are the words "spare,"
"delicate," "understated," or "low-fat."

I feel pretty sure that none of the recipes here are going to crop up any time
soon on the dessert menu of Chez Panisse—or Chez anywhere, for that matter.
But what you will find is laugh-out-loud fun—sometimes jaw-dropping, I-can't-
believe-we're-going-to-eat-that fun. These sweets are at home wherever a good
time is being had; from the beach boardwalk and the county fair to a birthday party
full of giggling children. Throw aside any fears about being gaudy, childish, or over-
the-top. There is candy, popcorn, and food-on-a-stick here! These are the desserts
to test the limits of your devotion to all good things sticky and sweet, gooey and
chewy. There is something here for everyone; from the tooth-aching sweetness
of honey-soaked baklava to warm, steamy biscuits soaked in a sticky, buttery
glaze studded with pecans to pastries so stuffed with coconut-perfumed
whipped cream you'll wish you could unhinge your jaw like a python
just to wrap your lips around it. So loosen up! Have a good
time! Smile. Go beyond tasteful and say hello to just
plain tasty.

This dessert is the perfect cure for the my-dog-died-my-boyfriend-dumped-me-I-hate-my-job-and-I'm-just-too-tired-to-chew blues. Cheesecake and ice cream—two delicious treats in one easy-to-drink creation. You can add a little fiber and vitamin C by throwing in a few strawberries (if you feel a twinge of conscience). I like to use wedges of Sara Lee's original cheesecake—store-bought is just fine. After all, if you are ready to prepare one of these beauties, it's obviously been one helluva day.

# New York Cheesecake Milkshake SOOTHES 2

1/2 CUP WHOLE MILK

2 WEDGES (4 TO 6 OUNCES EACH) PLAIN CHEESECAKE, STORE-BOUGHT OR HOMEMADE

1 TEASPOON PURE VANILLA EXTRACT

1 TO 2 PINTS PREMIUM VANILLA ICE CREAM

1/2 TO 3/4 CUP FRESH OR FROZEN STRAWBERRIES (OPTIONAL)

COMBINE THE MILK, cheesecake, vanilla, 1 pint of the ice cream, and the strawberries (if using) in a blender and purée until thick and smooth. If the mixture is too thin, add more ice cream a little bit at a time and blend. This milkshake should be thick enough to eat with a spoon if you like. Pour into 2 glasses, and enjoy with a very good friend.

*"I'm not a glutton—I am an explorer of food."*
—ERMA BOMBECK

Food on a stick just makes people smile. These adorable, chocolate-dipped bites of New York cheesecake are fun, and perfect party fare. I like to use wafer chocolate, or confectionery coating, for dipping the pops. Available in dark, milk, and white chocolate varieties, as well as a rainbow of colors, it doesn't need to be tempered and makes for easier dipping. To dress up your pops, you can roll them in crushed nuts, coarse sanding sugar, colorful jimmies, toffee bits, or mini chocolate chips, or drizzle them with a contrasting color of melted chocolate.

# Cheesecake Pops MAKES 30 TO 40 POPS

FIVE 8-OUNCE PACKAGES CREAM CHEESE, AT ROOM TEMPERATURE

2 CUPS SUGAR

1/4 CUP ALL-PURPOSE FLOUR

1/4 TEASPOON SALT

5 LARGE EGGS

2 EGG YOLKS

2 TEASPOONS PURE VANILLA EXTRACT

1/4 CUP HEAVY CREAM

BOILING WATER AS NEEDED

THIRTY TO FORTY 8-INCH LOLLIPOP STICKS

1 POUND SEMISWEET FLAVORED, MILK CHOCOLATE FLAVORED, OR BRIGHTLY COLORED CONFECTIONERY COATING (ALSO KNOWN AS SUMMER COATING OR WAFER CHOCOLATE)

POSITION AN OVEN RACK IN THE MIDDLE OF THE OVEN AND PREHEAT TO 325°F.

IN A LARGE BOWL, with an electric mixer set at low speed, beat together the cream cheese, sugar, flour, and salt until smooth. Add the whole eggs and the egg yolks, one at a time, beating well (but still at low speed) after each addition. Beat in the vanilla and cream.

LIGHTLY GREASE A 10-INCH CAKE PAN (NOT A SPRINGFORM PAN). Pour the cheesecake batter into the cake pan and place in a larger roasting pan. Fill the roasting pan with boiling water until it reaches halfway up the sides of the cake pan. Bake until the cheesecake is firm and slightly golden on top, 35 to 45 minutes.

REMOVE THE CHEESECAKE FROM THE WATER BATH AND COOL TO ROOM TEMPERATURE. Cover the cheesecake with plastic wrap and refrigerate until very cold, at least 3 hours or up to overnight.

WHEN COLD AND VERY FIRM, scoop the cheesecake into 2-ounce balls and place on a parchment paper–lined baking sheet. Carefully insert a lollipop stick into each cheesecake ball. Freeze the pops, uncovered, until very hard, at least 1 to 2 hours.

WHEN THE CHEESECAKE POPS ARE FROZEN AND READY FOR DIPPING, prepare the chocolate coating. Place half of the chocolate wafers in a microwave-safe bowl. Microwave on high for 30 seconds. Remove from the microwave and stir. If the chocolate is not completely melted, microwave for 30-second intervals, stirring until smooth.

QUICKLY DIP A FROZEN CHEESECAKE POP IN THE MELTED CHOCOLATE, swirling quickly to coat it completely. Hold the pop over the melted chocolate and shake off any excess. Place the pop on a clean parchment paper–lined baking sheet to set. Repeat with remaining pops, melting more chocolate wafers as needed.

REFRIGERATE THE POPS FOR UP TO 24 HOURS, until ready to serve.

In the depraved dessert hall of fame, deep-fried candy bars are king. Born in a Scottish fish-and-chips shop, brother to other brilliant culinary treasures such as the battered and deep-fried pickled egg and pizza slice, the deep-fried candy bar still reigns supreme. Equally at home in the food courts of county fairs across America, nestled between the fried onion blossoms and pork-chops-on-a-stick, or at the beach boardwalk next to cotton candy and salt-water taffy, nothing beats the visceral pleasure of biting into the crisp, crunchy shell, then the molten heart, of a deep-fried Milky Way. Most batters are thick pancake-style or funnel-cake batters, but this tempura-style batter yields a thin, crisp shell that barely encases the warm oozing center. Go ahead, just try one. It is sticky, gooey nirvana, for sure.

# Milky Way Tempura-on-a-Stick SERVES 6

6 FULL-SIZE (2.05 OUNCES EACH) MILKY WAY CANDY BARS

SIX 8-INCH LOLLIPOP STICKS

4 CUPS PEANUT OIL OR CANOLA OIL

**FOR THE BATTER:**

1 CUP RICE FLOUR

1/4 TEASPOON BAKING POWDER

PINCH OF SALT

1 EGG

1 CUP ICE COLD CLUB SODA

CONFECTIONERS' SUGAR FOR DUSTING

UNWRAP THE CANDY BARS AND INSERT THE LOLLIPOP STICKS LENGTHWISE INTO THEM. Refrigerate candy for at least 1 hour (for candy with a firmer center once fried, freeze the candy instead of refrigerating it).

FILL A DEEP-FRYER, large cast-iron skillet, or Dutch oven with the oil. Heat the oil to 365°F on a deep-frying thermometer.

WHILE THE OIL IS HEATING, MAKE THE BATTER: Sift the rice flour, baking powder, and salt into a shallow bowl. Make a well in the center of the flour and pour in the egg and club soda. Using a small wire whisk, quickly whisk all the ingredients together just until smooth. Hold the candy bars by their sticks and dip the chilled candy only into the batter, coating it completely. Gently shake off any excess batter.

FRY THE CANDY BARS, no more than 3 at a time and keeping the sticks out of the hot oil, until golden and crisp, turning once with metal tongs, 2 to 3 minutes total. Remove the candy from the hot oil and drain on a plate lined with paper towels. Dust with confectioners' sugar and let the candy cool for a moment or two before serving.

Nothing captures the attention of your taste buds like a little something deep-fried, a crackling crisp sheath of batter or bread crumbs giving way to the moist, sometimes gooey heart of flavor within. Fried food doesn't have to be heavy or oily; you just need to follow these three easy steps to ensure all your fried treats remain crunchy and grease-free.

### THE EQUIPMENT

A cast-iron skillet remains the tried-and-true work horse for frying. It's heavy and conducts and holds heat evenly. Woks and Dutch ovens are also a good choice because they, too, are heavy and their higher sides prevent the oil from splashing. Commercial fryers can be a good choice, but only if they can reach 365° to 375°F for optimum frying. Whatever your choice, make sure your pan is wide enough and deep enough to hold plenty of oil for frying. Foods actually fry up faster, lighter, crisper, and absorb less oil when surrounded by lots of hot oil as they cook. For safety, use a pan that is large enough to hold at least 8 to 12 cups of liquid. For the recipes in this book, you will only be using 3 to 4 cups of oil, but this allows plenty of room for the oil to bubble and splatter without being dangerous.

### THE OIL

Choose oil that can stand the heat. Peanut oil is my favorite. It can be heated up to 425°F before it starts to smoke and burn. Canola oil is another winner. It can't stand the same temperature as the peanut oil, but can certainly stand the temperatures needed to efficiently and safely fry most foods. Steer clear of olive oil for frying. Its strong flavor and low smoking point make it a poor choice—and a waste of such an expensive and flavorful ingredient.

### THE TEMPERATURE

The perfect temperature for optimum frying is 365° to 375°F. Fried foods will absorb too much oil if they are cooked in oil heated below 340°F. If the temperature rises above 375°F they will brown too quickly before the interiors are cooked through. The easiest way to monitor your temperature is with a deep-frying thermometer. If you don't have one, try the bread cube test: Cut a small cube of white bread and drop it in the hot oil. The bread will fry up golden brown in 1 minute at 350°F; at 375° it will take 40 seconds.

### ONE MORE TIP

After you have finished frying, let the oil cool completely before discarding it. It is best to discard the oil, as it can grow rancid quickly after its initial use.

## FEAR OF FRYING

*"Everything I want is either illegal, immoral, or fattening."*
—ALEXANDER WOOLLCOTT

When I was seven years old, my mother enrolled me in my first cooking class. I loved it, and learned how to make cinnamon rolls by dipping refrigerator biscuits in melted butter and rolling them in cinnamon-sugar and walnuts before baking. Delicious! My family gobbled them up and the compliments for my cooking made me beam. Those cinnamon biscuits became a Christmas breakfast tradition for many years. I've upgraded them here with homemade Southern biscuits sprinkled with cinnamon-sugar and baked atop a sticky, gooey pecan syrup. Simple, sweet, and easy, they are a perfect grown-up version of my childhood specialty.

# Quicky Sticky Biscuits MAKES ABOUT 12 BIG BISCUITS

**FOR THE STICKY PECAN SAUCE:**

1 CUP FIRMLY PACKED LIGHT BROWN SUGAR

1/2 CUP DARK CORN SYRUP

3/4 CUP (11/2 STICKS) UNSALTED BUTTER

11/2 CUPS CHOPPED PECANS OR WALNUTS, TOASTED (SEE PAGE 89)

**FOR THE BISCUITS:**

4 CUPS BLEACHED ALL-PURPOSE FLOUR

2 TABLESPOON BAKING POWDER

1/2 TEASPOONS BAKING SODA

11/2 TEASPOONS SALT

1 CUP (2 STICKS) VERY COLD OR FROZEN UNSALTED BUTTER, CUT INTO 16 PIECES

11/2 TO 2 CUPS COLD BUTTERMILK

**FOR THE TOPPING:**

1/2 CUP GRANULATED SUGAR

1 TEASPOON GROUND CINNAMON

1 STICK (4 OUNCES) UNSALTED BUTTER, MELTED

POSITION A RACK IN THE MIDDLE OF THE OVEN AND PREHEAT TO 425°F. Grease a 9-by-13-inch pan with softened butter or spray with nonstick cooking spray.

TO MAKE THE SAUCE: Combine the brown sugar, corn syrup, and butter. Melt over low heat. When the butter is melted, increase the heat to high and bring to a gentle boil. Cook, uncovered, until the mixture thickens, 3 to 5 minutes. Stir in the chopped nuts. Pour the mixture into the prepared pan and spread evenly. Set aside.

TO MAKE THE BISCUITS: In a large bowl, sift together twice the flour, baking powder, baking soda, and salt. Cut the butter into the flour mixture using a pastry cutter. Blend until most of the mixture looks like coarse crumbs, with some of the bits of butter the size of small peas.

MAKE A SHALLOW WELL IN THE CENTER OF THE FLOUR MIXTURE AND POUR IN 11/2 CUPS OF THE COLD BUTTERMILK. Use a fork to blend the buttermilk into the flour to create a soft dough. If the dough seems too dry as you are stirring it, add the remaining 1/2 cup buttermilk. Turn the dough out onto a lightly floured work surface and knead a few times to make sure it comes together. Pat the dough into a 3/4-inch-thick rectangle. Use a sharp chef's knife to cut the dough into 12 square biscuits.

TO MAKE THE TOPPING: In a small bowl, stir together the granulated sugar and cinnamon. Brush the tops of the biscuits with some of the melted butter and sprinkle with some of the cinnamon-sugar. Place the biscuits, evenly spaced, cinnamon-sugar-side down, into the pecan syrup–lined pan. Brush the tops (once the bottoms) of the biscuits with more melted butter and sprinkle with a little more cinnamon-sugar.

BAKE THE BISCUITS UNTIL GOLDEN BROWN AND PUFFY, and the sticky pecan sauce is bubbling around them, 15 to 17 minutes. Cool slightly, then place a large serving platter over the top of the pan and invert it. Remove the pan and allow the pecan sauce to fall around the biscuits. Use a small spatula to scrape any residual syrup from the pan onto the biscuits. Serve immediately.

Warm and buttery, soft and steaming: Who can resist a freshly baked, fat, golden biscuit? It takes a light hand and a deft touch to create the oh-so-simple, but often elusive, perfect biscuit. Biscuits are a member of the quick bread family, using baking powder, baking soda, or a combination of the two, as a leavening agent to help them rise. Biscuits can be made with butter, shortening, or lard for flakiness, and milk, buttermilk, or cream can be used to give them flavor and a moist, creamy crumb. Try these tips to ensure a biscuit that is light and tender.

- Measure your ingredients accurately.

- Make sure your fat and milk are very cold. Cut the fat into tiny pieces and then chill, or freeze, again until very firm before you cut it into the flour.

## BISCUIT BASICS

- Use fresh leavening agents. Use baking powder and baking soda that is very fresh; buy new cans if you have to—old, tired leavening agents contribute to old, tired biscuits.

- Use soft flour. Use either soft, Southern all-purpose flour (don't use self-rising unless the recipe calls for it) or standard, bleached all-purpose flour for tender biscuits.

- Don't overmix. When adding the liquid ingredients to the dry ingredients, make a well in the center of the flour/fat mixture and then pour the milk into the well. Use a fork to carefully blend them together, just until blended. The mixture may be lumpy, but that's fine.

- Knead gently. Pour the dough onto a lightly floured work surface (the dough should be soft and sticky), sprinkle lightly with flour, and knead gently just until the dough is combined. This is a gentle knead; really you are just helping the dough turn over on itself to combine, not kneading vigorously as you would bread dough. Use a flat plastic dough scraper and cool hands to help gently combine the dough. Remember to handle the dough as little as possible and keep the fat cold until it hits the hot oven.

- Pat, don't roll. Use your hands, not a rolling pin, to quickly and gently pat the dough into a flat rectangle about ½ inch to ¾ inch thick. Biscuits should at least double in height during baking.

- Don't twist the biscuit cutter. Dip your biscuit cutter in flour and make your cut in one swift, clean motion. If you twist the cutter, this will inhibit the biscuit from rising. For square biscuits, just cut dough with a sharp knife.

- Start cold and finish hot. Cold biscuits like a very hot oven. Make sure the oven is preheated to 400° to 450°F (depending on the recipe) and pop the biscuits in as soon as they are shaped. If it seems like the dough has been handled too much and the bits of fat have softened, chill the cut biscuits for 10 to 15 minutes before you bake them.

See's Candies are a California institution, and everyone has their favorites. I love Scotchmallows, a fat brown-sugar caramel topped with a chewy pillow of marshmallow and dipped in dark chocolate. These flavors are especially tempting when translated into an ice-cream sundae. In my favorite version, I dribble butterscotch and marshmallow sauces over dark chocolate ice cream, but you can also smother vanilla ice cream with a combination of the butterscotch sauce, dark chocolate, and marshmallow sauces. Top either combination with whipped cream and a generous sprinkling of chocolate jimmies.

# Scotchmallow Ice-Cream Sundae SERVES 4

**FOR THE BUTTERSCOTCH SAUCE:**

1 CUP FIRMLY PACKED DARK MUSCOVADO OR DARK BROWN SUGAR

4 TABLESPOONS UNSALTED BUTTER

2 TEASPOONS FRESH LEMON JUICE

1/2 TEASPOON SALT

1 CUP HEAVY CREAM

3 TABLESPOONS BOURBON

**FOR THE MARSHMALLOW SAUCE:**

1 JAR (7 1/2 OUNCES) MARSHMALLOW FLUFF

3 TO 4 TABLESPOONS BOILING WATER

1 QUART PREMIUM DARK CHOCOLATE ICE CREAM

SWEETENED WHIPPED CREAM (PAGE 43) FOR SERVING

CHOCOLATE JIMMIES FOR SPRINKLING

**TO MAKE THE BUTTERSCOTCH SAUCE:** Combine the brown sugar, butter, lemon juice, and salt in a heavy-bottomed saucepan and cook, stirring, until the butter melts and combines with the sugar. Increase the heat to high and cook, stirring occasionally, until the mixture is bubbling vigorously, 3 to 4 minutes. Stir in the cream, using a long-handled wooden spoon, as the hot sugar tends to hiss and splash as the cold cream hits it. Return the sauce to a boil and cook until thickened, 3 to 5 minutes longer. Remove from the heat and stir in the bourbon.

**TO MAKE THE MARSHMALLOW SAUCE:** Spoon the Fluff into a bowl and stir in 3 tablespoons of the boiling water to form a flowing sauce. If the sauce is too thick, add a little more water until it is a flowing consistency.

**TO ASSEMBLE THE SUNDAES,** place two 1/2-cup scoops of the chocolate ice cream in each of 4 glass dishes. Pour the warm butterscotch sauce over one scoop and the marshmallow sauce over the other. Top each sundae with whipped cream and a shower of chocolate jimmies. Serve immediately.

Giggling aside, this quick—and decidedly adult—dessert is a more solid version of a cocktail featuring crème de bananes and crème de cacao. Taking my initial cue from Bananas Foster, I've added a lush coffee note by dousing the buttery caramel bananas with Kahlúa and dark rum. Spooned over strong, bittersweet coffee ice cream and slathered with chocolate whipped cream, this dessert will satisfy on many levels.

# Dirty Banana Sundae SERVES 2

**FOR THE CHOCOLATE WHIPPED CREAM:**

1 CUP HEAVY CREAM

2 TO 3 TABLESPOONS DUTCH PROCESSED COCOA POWDER (SEE PAGE 45)

1/4 CUP CONFECTIONERS' SUGAR, SIFTED, PLUS MORE IF NEEDED

1/2 TEASPOON PURE VANILLA EXTRACT

**FOR THE DIRTY BANANAS:**

4 TABLESPOONS BUTTER

1 CUP FIRMLY PACKED LIGHT BROWN SUGAR

2 FIRM BARELY RIPE BANANAS

1/4 CUP KAHLÚA

1/4 CUP DARK RUM

4 LARGE SCOOPS PREMIUM COFFEE ICE CREAM

CHOCOLATE CURLS (PAGE 20) FOR GARNISH

**TO MAKE THE CHOCOLATE WHIPPED CREAM:** In a large bowl, combine the cream, cocoa powder, 1/4 cup confectioners' sugar, and vanilla and stir until smooth and the cocoa is dissolved. Refrigerate the chocolate cream for at least 1 hour to allow the chocolate flavor to blossom in the cream. Using an electric mixer set on medium speed, whip the cold cream until soft peaks form. Taste for sweetness, adding more confectioners' sugar to taste if you like, and continue beating for a few more seconds, just until the cream forms barely firm peaks.

**THE CHOCOLATE WHIPPED CREAM CAN BE STORED IN THE REFRIGERATOR FOR 1 FULL DAY.** (Make it in the morning to serve in the evening when you want few distractions.)

**TO MAKE THE BANANAS:** Combine the butter and brown sugar in a large sauté pan over medium heat, stirring occasionally, until the sugar and butter melt together into a bubbling syrup. While the syrup is cooking, slice the bananas on the diagonal into 1-inch-thick slices. Add the Kahlúa, stirring to combine, and then the bananas to the pan. Cook briefly and then add the rum. Bring the mixture to a boil and cook for 1 minute.

**REMOVE FROM THE HEAT AND SPOON THE WARM SAUCE OVER THE ICE CREAM,** serving 2 generous scoops per person. Top the ice cream and bananas with a large spoonful of the chocolate whipped cream and graze the top with a few chocolate curls. Serve immediately.

"And finally, monsieur, a wafer-thin mint." If you are a Monty Python fan, you may remember this line from the movie *And Now for Something Completely Different*. Eating that little wafer-thin mint didn't end well for Mr. Creosote (he exploded), but you will have far better luck with this make-it-yourself thin-mint ice-cream sundae. After Eight mints really are "wafer-thin," and their mint filling is soft and creamy, so they become chewy, not hard and waxy, when quickly blended and frozen with the ice cream. Topped with a rich, but refreshing, chocolate mint ganache sauce, this sundae is the perfect ending to a large or spicy meal.

# Wafer-Thin-Mint Sundae SERVES 4 TO 6
# with Bittersweet Peppermint Ganache

**FOR THE VANILLA-MINT ICE CREAM:**

25 AFTER EIGHT WAFER-THIN CHOCOLATE MINTS

1 QUART VERY FIRM PREMIUM VANILLA ICE CREAM

**FOR THE BITTERSWEET PEPPERMINT GANACHE:**

1 CUP HEAVY CREAM

8 OUNCES SEMISWEET OR BITTER-SWEET CHOCOLATE, FINELY CHOPPED

1/2 TO 1 TEASPOON PURE PEPPERMINT EXTRACT

MINT SPRIGS AND CHOCOLATE CURLS (PAGE 20) FOR GARNISH (OPTIONAL)

TO MAKE THE VANILLA-MINT ICE CREAM: Stack the mints in groups of 6 and cut each little stack of mint squares into quarters. Cut the cardboard container from the ice cream. On a clean cutting board, use a sharp chef's knife to cut the ice cream into 4 or 5 large chunks. Combine the ice cream and mints in the bowl of a stand mixer. Using the paddle attachment, beat together the mints and ice cream until combined. The ice cream should be creamy but firm and have chunks of mints and little flecks of chocolate throughout. Spoon the ice cream into a clean 1-quart container and freeze until firm enough to scoop.

WHEN READY TO SERVE, MAKE THE GANACHE: Pour the cream into a heavy-bottomed saucepan and bring just to a boil over medium heat. Remove the pan from the heat and sprinkle the chopped chocolate over the hot cream. Let the cream and chocolate stand for a minute, then stir gently until the chocolate melts completely and the sauce becomes silky and smooth. Add 1/2 teaspoon of the peppermint extract and stir until combined. Taste the sauce to judge the peppermint intensity and add up to 1/2 teaspoon more, if you prefer a stronger mint flavor.

TO SERVE, place 1 or 2 scoops of vanilla-mint ice cream in each dessert glass and cover with a ladle full of warm ganache. Garnish with a sprig of mint and a few chocolate curls, if desired, and serve.

My husband bought me a panini grill for Christmas this year, and I have a tremendous, if short-lived, love for all culinary gadgets. There are many elegant, sweet panini recipes that call for good artisanal bread and an elegant sliver of fine, dark chocolate, but I just couldn't help myself. Having just received a case of Marshmallow Fluff directly from the factory, I was compelled to experiment. Nothing goes better with Marshmallow Fluff than peanut butter and nothing goes better with peanut butter than milk chocolate. Why not stuff these three ultra-American ingredients into the moist, yeasty interior of a thoroughly French croissant? Despite the writhing agony of both Italian and French purists, there is a surprising symphony of tastes and textures here, from the flaky, buttery exterior of the croissant to the gooey, slightly savory, creamy sweetness of the melded chocolate-marshmallow-peanutty filling. Honey, this is one guilty pleasure you won't want to miss!

# White Trash Panini SERVES 1

(Lock the door, close the curtains, and turn over any copies of *Gourmet* magazine you may have in the house)

1 CROISSANT

2 TABLESPOONS CREAMY OR CHUNKY PEANUT BUTTER

1/2 FULL-SIZE HERSHEY'S MILK CHOCOLATE CANDY BAR (1.05 OUNCES)

3 TABLESPOONS MARSHMALLOW FLUFF

MELTED BUTTER FOR BRUSHING

CONFECTIONERS' SUGAR FOR SPRINKLING

HEAT A PANINI GRILL OR OTHER GRIDDLE TO MEDIUM HEAT. Use a serrated knife to split the croissant in half lengthwise. Spread one half with peanut butter. Break the chocolate into small squares and lay atop the peanut butter. Spread the Marshmallow Fluff on the remaining croissant half (the quantities of the filling ingredients are approximations—let the size of your croissant, and your appetite, be your guide). Press the sandwich together. Brush very lightly with melted butter. Press the croissant in the panini grill until it is slightly flattened and crisp and the filling is warm and melted, 4 to 5 minutes.

REMOVE YOUR CROISSANT FROM THE PANINI PRESS AND LET IT COOL SLIGHTLY. Sprinkle with confectioners' sugar. Use a serrated knife to cut in half. Eat immediately.

Move over, donuts; here come cream puffs. Cream puffs are experiencing a bit of a renaissance in popularity lately; companies like Beard Papa, the Japanese-born cream-puff company, ride the pâte à choux boom as their shops continue to expand across the country. With distinctive, creamy fillings in flavors from the classic vanilla and chocolate custard to green tea and mango, the cream puffs at Beard Papa showcase how versatile this old-fashioned pastry can be. In my opinion, you can never have too much cream in a cream puff; it should be so stuffed with cream that there is no dainty way to eat it. The messier the better! Sweetened cream of coconut and shredded coconut add a one-two punch of flavor in the whipped cream filling for these big, billowy puffs.

# Giant Coconut Cream Puffs MAKES 8 BIG CREAM PUFFS

**FOR THE CREAM PUFFS:**

1 CUP WATER

1/2 CUP UNSALTED BUTTER

1/2 TEASPOON SALT

2 TABLESPOONS SUGAR

1 1/4 CUPS UNBLEACHED ALL-PURPOSE FLOUR, SIFTED THEN MEASURED

4 TO 5 LARGE EGGS, PLUS 1 EGG BEATEN WITH 1 TABLESPOON WATER FOR BRUSHING

1/2 CUP SHREDDED SWEETENED COCONUT

**FOR THE FILLING:**

1 QUART HEAVY CREAM

1/2 CUP CONFECTIONERS' SUGAR, SIFTED

1/2 CUP CREAM OF COCONUT (SEE PAGE 78)

1 CUP SWEETENED SHREDDED COCONUT

CONFECTIONERS' SUGAR FOR DUSTING

POSITION A RACK ON THE BOTTOM SHELF OF THE OVEN AND PREHEAT TO 400°F. Use a nonstick baking sheet, or lightly grease a noninsulated aluminum baking sheet with solid shortening or butter and dust with flour. Turn the pan over and tap to remove any excess flour.

TO MAKE THE CREAM PUFFS: Combine the water, butter, salt, and sugar in a non-aluminum saucepan over medium heat and cook, stirring occasionally, until the butter melts completely. Do not allow the water to boil before the butter melts—this upsets the balance of moisture in the finished pastry.

INCREASE THE HEAT TO HIGH AND BRING THE MIXTURE TO A FULL, rolling boil. Remove the pan from the heat and add in the flour all at once, stirring briskly with a wooden spoon until the dough pulls away from the sides of the pan and gathers in a clump around the spoon. Return the pan to medium heat and stir the batter briskly for 30 to 60 seconds. This will dry out any excess moisture and eliminate any raw flour taste from the dough.

LINE YOUR COUNTERTOP WITH A LARGE PIECE OF ALUMINUM FOIL AND TURN THE DOUGH OUT ONTO THE FOIL. Pat the dough into an 8-inch circle and let cool for 5 minutes. (If the batter is too hot, the eggs will start cooking before the pastry is baked, and the puffs won't be as crisp and light as they should be.) Return the dough to the saucepan.

CRACK 4 OF THE EGGS INTO A BOWL AND BEAT WITH A FORK UNTIL BLENDED. Add one-fourth of the beaten egg to the dough, stirring slowly so that the dough, which will become slippery with the addition of the egg, doesn't slop out of the pan. As the egg is incorporated into the dough, stir more briskly. When the batter smooths out, add another one-fourth of the beaten eggs. Repeat until all the beaten eggs have been incorporated into the dough. The final batter should be smooth, slightly sticky, and malleable but firm enough to form soft peaks and be piped or spooned onto a baking sheet. If the batter seems too firm, beat the fifth egg with a fork and add it to the batter, 1 tablespoon at a time, until it reaches the right consistency. Do not add too much egg—if the batter is too runny, the puffs won't rise properly.

DIVIDE THE BATTER INTO 8 SCOOPS, spacing them 2 to 3 inches apart on the prepared baking sheet. Brush each dollop of batter with a little egg wash and sprinkle each with 1 tablespoon of the shredded coconut. Bake until the puffs are golden brown and expanded to 3 times their original size, 20 to 25 minutes. Reduce the oven temperature to 350°F and continue baking for 15 minutes to make sure the pastry is crisp, hollow, and dry inside. Transfer to a wire rack to cool.

USING A SERRATED KNIFE, gently saw the puffs in half horizontally. This will release any steam trapped within the puffs that can make them soggy. Place the split puffs back on the baking sheet and return to the oven for 3 minutes. Remove from the oven and let cool completely. The cream puffs are best filled as close to serving time as possible, but they can be filled and refrigerated up to 4 hours before serving.

TO MAKE THE FILLING: Place a large mixing bowl and mixer beaters in the freezer for 15 minutes to chill. Combine the cream, confectioners' sugar, and coconut cream in the chilled bowl and beat using an electric mixer set at medium-low speed, until the cream starts to thicken. Increase the mixer speed to medium and beat until the cream nearly doubles in volume and forms soft peaks. Use a large balloon whisk to fold in the shredded coconut and continue beating by hand until stiff peaks form.

FIT A LARGE PASTRY BAG WITH A LARGE STAR TIP AND FILL WITH THE WHIPPED COCONUT-CREAM FILLING. Pipe 1 cup of the filling into the bottom half of each puff, generously mounding it above the edge of the shell. Alternatively, use a spoon to mound the filling into the cream puff shell. Set the top of each cream puff (like a hat) on top of the mounded whipped cream. Dust with the confectioners' sugar and serve.

There is no satisfaction sweeter than mastering the simple art of preparing pâte à choux. What other combination of water, fat, flour, and eggs yields such eye-popping results? Pâte à choux can morph from a little blob of dough into so many tasty and elegant creations. Piped onto a baking sheet and popped into a hot oven, dollops of this pastry bake into crisp, airy globes you can stuff with mounds of whipped cream for cream puffs, fill with custard and glaze with chocolate for éclairs, or split open and fill with ice cream and drizzle with warm chocolate sauce for profiteroles. Pop strips of pâte à choux into hot oil and it transforms into sizzling crisp, eggy churros just waiting to be rolled in sweet and spicy cinnamon-sugar and dunked in bath of deep, rich hot chocolate.

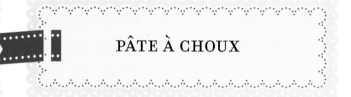

## PÂTE À CHOUX

Follow these simple steps for perfect pâte à choux:

- *Melt, then boil.* Don't let the water start to boil before the butter melts. If it boils too soon, it will disrupt the balance of moisture in the finished pastry.

- *Add the flour all at once.* As soon as the water comes to a rolling boil, remove from the heat and add the flour all at once. Stir like mad with a wooden spoon until it forms a dough that pulls away from the sides the pan.

- *Dry the dough.* Cook the dough for an additional 30 to 60 seconds to eliminate any raw flour taste in your dough. A drier dough will also absorb more egg for a lighter, crisper pastry.

- *Cool, then beat.* Make sure to let the dough cool for about 5 minutes before adding the eggs—any less and the eggs will start cooking in the dough before the pastries are baked. But don't let it cool too long, or the dough will not be able to absorb the correct amount of beaten egg. Either way, your puffs will flop.

- *A little at a time.* Beat in the eggs, a little at a time. The final batter should be smooth and glossy and a little sticky, but firm enough to hold its shape without being runny or oozing.

- *Bake high down low.* Start baking your pastry at a hot 400°F on the lowest rack of the oven. Your pâte à choux will triple in volume when it gets this direct blast of heat. Reduce the heat after about 20 minutes and continue baking until your puffs are golden brown and crisp.

- *Release the steam.* When the pastries are completely cooked, pierce each one with a wooden skewer to release the steam that could make them soggy. Let cool slightly and then return to the oven again for 3 to 4 minutes to completely dry out the interior. The filled puffs will remain crisper longer if you follow this final step.

*"How long does getting thin take?" asked Pooh anxiously.*
—FROM WINNIE-THE-POOH, BY A. A. MILNE

My daughters and I stood for a long time in front of the picture window at Winnie-the-Pooh's Candy Kitchen in Disneyland, watching the candy makers as they threaded marshmallows onto skewers and then dipped them into thick, gooey caramel. They were lined up to cool—glossy caramel soldiers—waiting to be plunged into a big vat of melted chocolate. I find excess like this endlessly mesmerizing. Sophia, my connoisseur of all things marshmallow, liked the ones dipped in orange confectionery coating and drizzled with dark chocolate to resemble Tigger's tail.

# Heaven-on-a-Stick MAKES 12 LITTLE STICKS OF HEAVEN

36 TO 48 LARGE MARSHMALLOWS

12 BAMBOO SKEWERS

1 CAN (14 OUNCES) SWEETENED CONDENSED MILK

4 TABLESPOONS (1/2 STICK) UNSALTED BUTTER

1/4 TEASPOON SALT

1 TEASPOON PURE VANILLA EXTRACT

1 BAG (14 OUNCES) CARAMEL CANDIES (ABOUT 50 INDIVIDUAL CARAMELS), UNWRAPPED

1 POUND SEMISWEET OR MILK CHOCOLATE-FLAVORED CONFECTIONERY COATING, MELTED

CHOPPED NUTS

MINI CANDY-COATED CHOCOLATE PIECES SUCH AS M&M'S

COLORED OR CHOCOLATE SPRINKLES

CHOCOLATE SANDWICH COOKIE CRUMBS

MELTED WHITE CHOCOLATE (SEE PAGE 21) FOR DRIZZLING

THREAD 3 OR 4 MARSHMALLOWS ONTO EACH SKEWER. Line a baking sheet with parchment paper and spray lightly with nonstick cooking spray.

COMBINE THE CONDENSED MILK, butter, salt, and vanilla in a large saucepan over medium heat and cook until the butter melts and combines with the milk. Bring to a boil and cook, stirring constantly, for 1 minute. Stir in the caramels and cook, stirring constantly, until the caramels melt and mixture is smooth. Reduce the heat to low and simmer the caramel, stirring, for 1 minute longer. Remove from the heat and dip the skewers of marshmallows into the caramel, rolling them around and coating them completely. Holding each skewer over the pan, shake off any excess caramel. Place the dipped marshmallow skewers on the prepared baking sheet and store in the freezer until the caramel hardens and the skewer is easily lifted from the parchment, about 30 minutes.

WHEN THE CARAMEL HAS HARDENED AROUND THE MARSHMALLOWS, dip them in the melted chocolate coating, then roll them in chopped nuts or candy pieces, sprinkles, or cookie crumbs as you like. Refrigerate the skewers until the chocolate coating hardens, 10 to 15 minutes. Alternatively, you can skip the candy or nut coating altogether and instead allow the dark chocolate coating to cool and harden, then drizzle the skewers with melted white chocolate.

THESE LITTLE SKEWERS CAN BE REFRIGERATED FOR UP TO 1 WEEK, or packaged in cellophane bags and tied with a ribbon, for giving. For children's birthday parties, fill brightly colored metal buckets with florist foam to hold your marshmallow sticks and then fill the bucket with mini jelly beans or other small candies to cover the foam. A huge hit!

If you look hard enough, it seems every culture has some little guilty-pleasure-in-a-jar that captivates the imagination and palate of its citizens and turns ordinary people into enthusiastic, even rabid and perhaps slightly gluttonous, fans. These sweet treats are easy to eat and easy to find, and at some point have all been eaten alone with a spoon or licked from fingers when no one is looking. They sit innocuously in the back of the fridge or on the pantry shelf with all the other staples, as much a part of daily life as milk and bread.

### DULCE DE LECHE

Häagen-Dazs may have made *dulce de leche* a household name to the American public in 1997 when they introduced their new ice cream flavor, but *dulce de leche* was already a national obsession and an everyday staple in Argentina, Uruguay, Brazil, Chile, and other South American countries. Literally translated

## GUILTY PLEASURES IN A JAR

as "milk sweet" or "milk jam," *dulce de leche* is hugely popular all over South America with children and adults for its thick, gooey, texture. There are shelves devoted to *dulce de leche* in the grocery store, and shoppers can buy it in containers as large as 1 or 2 liters. *Dulce de leche* is used to spread on buttered toast, or between layers of cake, as a filling in tarts and turnovers, or to sandwich together meringues or delicate little butter cookies called *alfajores*. Mexico's version of *dulce de leche*, called *cajeta*, combines goat's milk and cow's milk for a rich, subtle tang that is equally delicious. Unlike butterscotch or caramel, where the sugars are caramelized first before cream is added, both *cajeta* and *dulce de leche* are made by boiling milk and sugar down together until they become a gooey, thick, almost fudgey golden paste, with a distinctive milky, caramelized flavor. Most modern recipes now recommend reducing sweetened condensed milk until it thickens into the familiar creamy, spreadable confection.

You can make *dulce de leche* yourself, and many recipes call for boiling unopened cans of sweetened condensed milk for hours to achieve the perfect consistency. But if you are easily distracted and tend to forget to do things like clean out the lint screen in your dryer, or habitually leave your curling iron plugged in for hours at a time, or other nasty habits that will make your local firefighters blanch, you may balk at a recipe that can cause an explosion if the water level in your pot gets too low. Instead, pour the sweetened condensed milk (I like to add a few drops of vanilla and a pinch of salt) into a glass pie pan and cover tightly with aluminum foil. Place the pie pan in a roasting pan and fill with boiling water until it reaches halfway up the sides of the pie pan. Bake for 1 to 2 hours in a 400° to 425°F oven until the milk is very thick and jammy and a rich, golden brown. This method may not be as thrillingly dangerous, but it is much less stressful, and all small children, pets, and clean ceilings in your home will thank you.

### HERSHEY'S CHOCOLATE SYRUP

When I was growing up, everyone I knew always had a little can full of Hershey's chocolate syrup chilling in the door of their refrigerator. Usually dripping a sticky black goo of dribbled chocolate, there was something comforting in the familiar presence of that squat brown can. Hershey's syrup was created in 1926 and introduced to the general public in 1928, and remains at the heart of many favorite ice-cream-fountain treats. From chocolate sodas and egg creams to chocolate Cokes and the infamous Black Cow soda featuring root beer, vanilla ice cream, and chocolate syrup, Hershey's chocolate syrup made a huge impression on my developing chocolate palate. My favorite Sunday-night treat was sitting in front of the television at 7:00 P.M. for *The Wonderful World of Disney* with a big bowl of vanilla ice cream doused in chocolate syrup. Sometimes we added sliced bananas, but usually it was just ice cream and syrup. You never ate it straight up—the proper method was to stir the ice cream and chocolate syrup together until it achieved just the right gooey, Dairy Queen soft-serve consistency. You then had to eat it at just the right speed, a tricky business because if eaten too slowly, the ice cream lost that luscious, supple creaminess and started to melt, but if you were too greedy and ate it too fast, that all-too-familiar icy knot of pain hit right behind your eye—brain freeze.

My mother taught me how to make the perfect chocolate milkshake. She insisted a proper chocolate shake was never made with chocolate ice cream, but could only be achieved using vanilla ice cream, a generous portion of that thick-as-crude-oil chocolate syrup, and the merest splash of milk. Into the blender went a little milk, then a hefty squirt of syrup followed by large scoops of ice cream. The mix was blended in loud pulses and tested for the right level of chocolate flavor. Mom's milkshakes were never too thin or too thick. I have to admit, her milkshakes were the best: thick and spoonable, creamy, and intensely chocolaty. Milkshakes made with chocolate ice cream alone still seem gray and pallid by comparison.

### MARSHMALLOW FLUFF

Anyone who has enjoyed a gooey piece of Marshmallow Fluff fudge or a simple "Fluffernutter" is well versed in the deliciously sticky charms of Marshmallow Fluff. There are other marshmallow cremes on the market, but none have the same light, fluffy texture of the classic Marshmallow Fluff. The recipe for Fluff was invented in Massachusetts by Archibald Query and sold door-to-door before sugar rationing during World War I forced him to close up shop. When sugar flowed freely again during the 1920s, manufacturing the sweet treat no longer held the same allure, so Query sold his secret recipe to two young WWI veterans, H. Allen Durkee and Fred L. Mower, for $500—a steep price in that day. But Durkee and Mower had a vision, and soon they too were peddling this addictive treat door to door. The two men named their marshmallow treat "Toot Sweet Marshmallow Fluff," but later shortened the name to Marshmallow Fluff. Popularity for their confection continued to grow, and soon jars of Fluff were lining grocers' shelves. As the years went by, Fluff became even more popular, and in the 1930s Marshmallow Fluff even sponsored a musical-comedy radio show featuring the singing sensations the Flufferettes. Fluff making took another forced holiday due to more sugar rationing during WWII, but the small, family-run company was soon back in business with a state-of-the-art factory that has been whipping up batches using the same recipe Archibald Query invented ever since. Fluffernutter sandwiches—a mixture of peanut butter and Fluff between two slices of white bread—became the stuff of New England school-lunch legend and now, after its creation more than eighty years

ago, in most New England pantries, right next to the jar of peanut butter, sits a jar of Marshmallow Fluff. The company produced a small cookbook titled *The Yummy Book*, first published in 1930 and now in its ninth edition, detailing all the different uses for Marshmallow Fluff, from meringues and cheesecakes and fudge to cake frostings and fillings and gooey ice cream sauces.

Although a regional phenomenon in New England, Marshmallow Fluff has found its way into Canada, England, Europe, Australia, Israel, and South Africa. It hasn't, however, really traveled west of the Rockies, and Westerners must order their Fluff directly from the company to satisfy their craving for this airy, sticky-sweet confection.

### NUTELLA

Italian Nutella, a creamy, chocolate-hazelnut confection in a jar, was created by Pietro Ferrero, a Piedmontese baker who found himself with a shortage of chocolate and an abundance of local hazelnuts after World War II. To stretch his supply of chocolate, he mixed cocoa with sugar and ground hazelnut butter and created *pasta gianduja*. His new invention was a hit, and eventually his little jars of *Supercrema Gianduja* were gracing the pantries of households across Italy. Smeared on toast or croissants, swirled into ice cream, or eaten from the jar with a spoon, Ferrero's confection became a part of everyday life. It became so popular, neighborhood food stores started to keep a big jar on the counter and school children would run in with pieces of toasted bread and buy a "smear" for a few lire as an afternoon snack. In 1964, looking to expand their market, the Ferrero company renamed their chocolate-hazelnut treat Nutella, and a legend was born. It seems Italian university students are obsessed with Nutella, and live on it during exam time. There are Nutella fan clubs. Nutella is as common in European kitchens as peanut butter is in American kitchens. In fact, Nutella is more popular around the world than all brands of peanut butter combined.

It's Saturday morning. No one is up but you and the Cap'n, on the couch with SpongeBob. What could be better? How about these crisp, jarringly sweet nuggets melded together with melted marshmallows into a devilishly good, crispy treat? My daughter, Sophia, has considered marshmallows a perfectly sane breakfast choice since she was three, so, for her, these are brunch.

# Cap'n Crunch Crispy Treats MAKES 15 BARS

1 BOX (18 OUNCES) CAP'N CRUNCH CEREAL

6 TABLESPOONS BUTTER

1 BAG (16 OUNCES) MARSHMALLOWS

1/2 TEASPOON PURE VANILLA EXTRACT

PINCH OF SALT

GREASE A 9-BY-13-INCH BAKING PAN WITH SOFTENED BUTTER OR SPRAY WITH NONSTICK COOKING SPRAY.

POUR THE CEREAL INTO A LARGE BOWL AND SET ASIDE. Melt the butter in a large sauce-pan over low heat. Add the marshmallows, vanilla, and salt and cook, stirring constantly, until the marshmallows are melted into the butter. Immediately pour the marshmallow mixture over the cereal and stir with a large wooden spoon until all the cereal is coated with melted marshmallow.

SPOON THE CEREAL MIXTURE INTO THE PREPARED PAN. With buttered hands, gently but firmly press the cereal into the pan to compact the mixture. Let the mixture cool completely. When cool, cut into 15 large bars. Serve right away, or wrap each bar separately with waxed paper or plastic wrap and store in covered container for up to 2 days.

Make sure to prepare pralines on a warm, dry day. Moisture and humidity can turn tender, brown-sugar-sweet, fudgy pralines into sticky little puddles of goo.

# Creamy Pecan Pralines MAKES 16 PRALINES

1¹/2 CUPS GRANULATED SUGAR

1¹/2 CUPS PACKED DARK BROWN SUGAR

¹/2 TEASPOONS SALT

2 TABLESPOONS LIGHT CORN SYRUP

1 CUP HEAVY CREAM

3 TABLESPOONS UNSALTED BUTTER, AT ROOM TEMPERATURE AND CUT INTO BITS

2 TEASPOONS PURE VANILLA EXTRACT

2 CUPS PECAN HALVES, TOASTED (SEE PAGE 89) AND COOLED

2 TABLESPOONS BOURBON OR TENNESSEE WHISKEY (OPTIONAL; SEE PAGE 53)

LINE 2 BAKING SHEETS WITH PARCHMENT PAPER.

SPRAY THE SIDES OF A HEAVY 2-QUART SAUCEPAN WITH NONSTICK COOKING SPRAY. Combine the granulated sugar, brown sugar, salt, corn syrup, and cream and in the pan. Heat slowly over low heat, stirring constantly, until the sugars are melted and the mixture is smooth. Increase the heat to medium-high and bring the mixture to a boil. Boil gently until the mixture reaches the soft-ball stage (about 236°F on a candy thermometer; see page 154), about 5 minutes. Remove from heat and let the mixture cool until it reaches 220°F, about 10 minutes.

USING A WOODEN SPOON, beat in butter and vanilla until the mixture turns creamy and opaque. Stir in the pecans and whiskey, if using. Drop in ¹/4-cup portions on the prepared baking sheets. Let the pralines cool completely until firm. When cool, serve immediately, or wrap each praline individually in plastic wrap or waxed paper and store in a tightly covered container for up to 1 week.

These cookies are big and chewy with an aromatic blend of spices. The gingery bite of the cookies is a delicious contrast to the caramel sweetness of the ice cream. These are a great do-ahead dessert choice (my favorite kind) for a warm-weather family gathering, served along with Sticky Fingers Triple-Chocolate Ice-Cream Sandwiches (page 47). Children and adults will love them with equal zest. Feel free to substitute vanilla ice cream for the Dulce de Leche flavor here; just make sure to purchase the best brand of ice cream possible to go with your cookies.

# Gingersnap Dulce de Leche Ice-Cream Sandwiches MAKES 18 ICE CREAM SANDWICHES

1 CUP UNSALTED BUTTER, AT ROOM TEMPERATURE

1 CUP FIRMLY PACKED LIGHT BROWN SUGAR

1 CUP GRANULATED SUGAR

½ CUP MOLASSES

2 LARGE EGGS

4 CUPS UNBLEACHED ALL-PURPOSE FLOUR

2 TEASPOONS GROUND CINNAMON

1 TABLESPOON GROUND GINGER

½ TEASPOON GROUND CLOVES

¼ TEASPOON GROUND WHITE PEPPER

½ TEASPOON BAKING SODA

¼ TEASPOON SALT

DEMERARA SUGAR OR GRANULATED SUGAR FOR ROLLING

1 QUART PREMIUM DULCE DE LECHE ICE CREAM, SOFTENED

IN A LARGE BOWL, using an electric mixer set at medium speed, cream the butter, brown sugar, and granulated sugar together until light and fluffy. Add the molasses and eggs and beat until blended; the mixture may appear curdled at this point.

IN A MEDIUM BOWL, sift together the flour, cinnamon, ginger, cloves, white pepper, baking soda, and salt. Beat the dry ingredients into the wet ingredients just until they form a soft dough. Cover and refrigerate the dough for at least 2 hours or up to overnight.

POSITION A RACK IN THE MIDDLE OF THE OVEN AND PREHEAT TO 350°F. Line 2 baking sheets with parchment paper. Scoop the dough into thirty-six ¼-cup portions and roll into balls. Place the demerara sugar in a large shallow plate. Roll the dough balls liberally in the demerara sugar and place 2 inches apart (about 9 cookies per sheet) on the prepared baking sheets. Flatten slightly with the bottom of a glass. Bake, one sheet at a time, until the cookies are flattened and crackled and smell very spicy and fragrant, 11 to 14 minutes. Let cool for 5 minutes on the baking sheet before removing to a wire rack to cool completely. Repeat with clean parchment paper to bake the remaining cookies.

PLACE A LARGE SCOOP OF ICE CREAM ON THE BOTTOM OF ONE COOKIE, spreading the ice cream slightly to cover. Top with another cookie, pressing the bottom of the cookie onto the ice cream. Give the sandwich a gentle squeeze to compress the ice cream and cookies together. Serve immediately, or wrap each sandwich in plastic wrap or waxed paper and store in the freezer until you are ready to serve. These ice cream sandwiches can be made up to 1 day in advance of serving. Right before serving, roll the edges of the ice cream sandwich in demerara sugar, if desired.

A candy thermometer is fairly foolproof, but you can also use this old-fashioned, tried-and-true ice water test to gauge the temperature of your candy syrup.

- Have a glass of very cold ice water available for each test.

- Before you begin, remove the pan from the heat so the temperature doesn't continue to rise while you are testing your syrup.

- Pour a small spoonful of syrup into the cold water. The consistency of the syrup in the cold water reveals the texture your finished candy would have at this stage.

## TESTING CANDY

### SOFT-BALL STAGE (235°–240°F)

The syrup forms a soft, flexible ball at this stage. If you remove it from the water, it will hold its shape for a moment before it oozes slightly and flattens.

Fudge and pralines are both cooked to the soft-ball stage. These candies have a creamy texture that may spread a little while hot, but firm up as they cool.

### FIRM-BALL STAGE (245°–250°F)

The syrup forms a firm ball at this stage. When removed from the water it will hold its shape, but remain malleable. It will not flatten unless pressed or squeezed.

Caramels are cooked to the firm-ball stage. These candies are soft, but chewy, and sometimes a little sticky. They hold their shape and can be individually wrapped.

### HARD-BALL STAGE ( 250°–265°F)

At this stage the hot syrup will be thicker and will drop in fat threads from the spoon into the water. When the syrup hits the cold water, it will form a hard ball. It will not lose its shape when handled. Its shape can be changed by pressing or squeezing, but not as easily as syrup cooked to the firm-ball stage.

Nougat, marshmallow, and divinity are cooked to the hard-ball stage. These candies are firm and chewy and may often have a fairly dry exterior with a soft spongy center.

### SOFT-CRACK STAGE (270°–290°F)

At this stage, the hot sugar syrup will be very thick as more and more of the water is cooked away. When the syrup is dropped into the cold water it will solidify into firm yet flexible threads instead of a ball. The threads will hold their shape, but can be bent without breaking or snapping.

Salt water taffy and other very firm, very chewy, candies are cooked to the soft-crack stage.

### HARD-CRACK STAGE (300°–310°F)

Syrups cooked to this stage have very little water remaining in the mixture. A little syrup dropped in cold water will immediately harden into brittle threads that break easily when handled. Since the sugar syrup is so hot at this stage, allow the test to cool slightly in the cold water before touching it.

Toffee, brittles, and lollipops are cooked to the hard-crack stage. These candies are hard and crunchy. They can be poured into molds and will retain their shape when cool.

This reminds me of one of my favorite See's candies—cashew brittle. My husband insists that a See's candy store is one of the happiest places on earth, because the longer you linger, the more samples they will usually give you. I like using salted cashews here to give this crunchy candy its delectable sweet and salty savor.

# Salted Cashew Toffee MAKES ABOUT 2 POUNDS

1¼ CUPS (2½ STICKS) UNSALTED BUTTER

2 TABLESPOONS WATER

2 CUPS SUGAR

½ TEASPOON FRESH LEMON JUICE

½ TEASPOON BAKING SODA

¾ TEASPOON SALT

2 HEAPING CUPS SALTED CASHEW HALVES

SPRAY A LARGE BAKING SHEET WITH NONSTICK COOKING SPRAY.

IN A LARGE SAUCEPAN, combine the butter, water, sugar, and lemon juice. Cook over medium-low heat, stirring constantly, until the butter is melted. Increase the heat to high and bring to a boil, stirring constantly with a wooden spoon. When the mixture starts to boil, stop stirring and cook until the mixture reaches the hard-crack stage (about 300°F; see facing page), 5 to 8 minutes.

IMMEDIATELY REMOVE THE PAN FROM THE HEAT AND STIR IN THE BAKING SODA, salt, and the cashews. The syrup will boil and puff up when the baking soda is added—just keep stirring until it simmers down. (Adding baking soda aerates the syrup for a crisp, light-textured candy that won't break your tooth when you bite into it.) Pour the candy mixture onto the prepared baking sheet. Using a rubber spatula, work quickly as the candy cools to spread it into an approximately 9-by-13-inch rectangle, keeping the nuts in a single layer. Set the baking sheet on a wire rack and let the candy cool completely. When the candy is hard, break it into medium-size pieces to serve.

## VARIATION

BREAK THE CANDY INTO BITE-SIZE PIECES. Dip the toffee into melted white chocolate (see page 21) and place on parchment paper–lined baking sheets to harden. Serve, or package into small cellophane bags for gift giving.

Perfect for breakfast, brunch, or dessert, these slightly crisp, butter-fried, tart-at-the-center sandwiches are a snap to assemble if you have the filling chilled and ready to go before you start assembling them. Tangy, ruby-pink stalks of rhubarb combine with raspberry jam for a cool, sweet-and-sour filling that seeps into the heart of the feathery-light brioche. The panko, or Japanese bread crumbs, give these sandwiches a crisp, flaky crunch that serves as a delightful counterpoint to the moist, eggy bread underneath.

# Raspberry-Rhubarb Monte Cristo Sandwiches

SERVES 6

1/2 POUND RHUBARB

3/4 CUP GRANULATED SUGAR

1/2 CUP RASPBERRY JAM

1 1/2 CUPS HALF-AND-HALF

6 LARGE EGGS

2 TEASPOONS PURE VANILLA EXTRACT

1/4 TEASPOON SALT

ONE 13-OUNCE LOAF BRIOCHE OR CHALLAH BREAD

4 TABLESPOONS UNSALTED BUTTER

4 TABLESPOONS PEANUT OR OTHER VEGETABLE OIL

3 CUPS PANKO BREAD CRUMBS

CONFECTIONERS' SUGAR FOR DUSTING

SWEETENED WHIPPED CREAM (PAGE 43) OR VANILLA ICE CREAM (OPTIONAL)

COMBINE THE RHUBARB AND 1/2 CUP OF THE GRANULATED SUGAR IN A SMALL SAUCEPAN. Cook over medium heat, stirring occasionally, until the rhubarb is tender, and dissolves into a loose purée as you stir it. Remove from the heat and stir in the raspberry jam. Let cool completely.

IN A LARGE BOWL, combine the half-and-half, eggs, vanilla, salt, and remaining 1/4 cup granulated sugar. Whisk together until smooth. Pour the batter into a large shallow dish and set aside.

POSITION A RACK IN THE MIDDLE OF THE OVEN AND PREHEAT TO 350°F.

SLICE THE BRIOCHE CROSSWISE INTO SIX 2-INCH-THICK SLICES. With a small, sharp knife, cut a deep pocket into each piece of brioche, starting at the top of the slice—as if you are going to cut the thick piece into two 1-inch-thick slices, opening the bread up, but leaving the sides connected and not cutting all the way through to the bottom. Gently open each pocket, taking care not to rip the bread, and spoon 2 or 3 tablespoons of the rhubarb mixture into each slice of brioche. Dip 2 or 3 of the sandwiches into the batter and let soak for about 1 minute per side.

MELT 2 TABLESPOONS OF BUTTER AND 2 TABLESPOONS OIL IN A LARGE, nonstick skillet over medium heat. When the fats are melted and start to bubble, lift the sandwiches from the batter, allowing any excess to drip off, coat each side in the panko crumbs and place in the hot skillet. Cook until golden brown, 2 to 3 minutes per side. Place each sandwich on an ungreased baking sheet. Wipe out the used butter and oil from the frying pan with a paper towel and melt the remaining butter and oil over medium heat. Cook the remaining 3 sandwiches as you did the first batch. Place all 6 sandwiches on the ungreased baking sheet and bake for 5 to 6 minutes. Serve warm, sliced on the diagonal, sprinkled with confectioners' sugar, and accompanied by whipped cream or ice cream, if desired.

When I think of dates, sometimes I envision Moroccan kings, hot deserts, and the cool plip-plopping of water burbling into rose petal–strewn fountains. But usually, I think of my maternal great-grandmother. Grammie was an industrious and frugal woman until the day she died at age ninety-eight. Most gifts she gave were homemade, like the crazy-quilt pot holders she crocheted for my mother, crafted from assorted yarn scraps using old garter-belt rings to hang them from. More popular were the stuffed dates she sometimes made for us. They are surprisingly elegant little mouthfuls, perfectly at home among more elaborate sweets. I like to use fat, succulent Medjool dates for these simple treats. Considered the Cadillac of dates among growers, their creamy, candy-sweet flesh contrasts beautifully with the chunky, crunchy walnuts stuffed inside.

# Sugared Stuffed Dates  MAKES 2 DOZEN STUFFED DATES

2 DOZEN DATES, PREFERABLY MEDJOOL

ABOUT 4 DOZEN WALNUT HALVES, TOASTED (SEE PAGE 89) AND COOLED

1/2 CUP SUGAR

USING A SMALL PARING KNIFE, slice each date open lengthwise without cutting it completely in half and remove the pit. Break each walnut half in half again lengthwise and stuff the pieces into the cavities of the dates left by the pits. I like to stuff as many walnuts into the date as I can, and usually the soft, pliant flesh of the Medjool can accommodate at least 4 walnut quarters. Press the date closed around the nut filling. It's all right if the nut remains visible; you just want the date wrapped around the filling well enough to hold it captive.

PLACE THE SUGAR IN A SHALLOW BOWL. Roll each stuffed date in the sugar and place on a serving plate. Keep the dates covered until ready to serve.

In India, some Hindu gods feed on nothing else; Cupid, the mythic Roman god of love, dipped his arrows in it to sweeten the hearts of lovers; jars of it were entombed with the bodies of Egyptian pharaohs to ease their journey into the afterlife; and in ancient Rome, an offering of this liquid gold was enough to appease and calm the anger of many a disgruntled god. Honey. Thick, lustrous and golden, fragrant and deliciously sweet, honey has held mankind in its thrall for more than ten thousand years. Numerous civilizations have cherished the hard-working honey bee and revered honey itself as a symbol for all that is beautiful, good, and sweet in life. The industrious image of the honey bee is not unwarranted. They are responsible for pollinating most of our crops of fruits and vegetables. Honey bees must collect the nectar of two million flowers and travel thousands of miles to create one pound of honey, and the average honey bee will produce only $1/12$ teaspoon of honey in her entire lifetime. With medicinal, religious, and cosmetic as well as culinary uses, the ancient, sticky, trail of honey is seen and felt in many cultures throughout history.

### HONEY IN THE KITCHEN

Honey comes in as many varieties as there are flowers, from sage, clover, lavender, and orange blossom honey to heather, chestnut, leatherwood, and thyme blossom varieties, among many others. In general, the lighter in color the honey, the milder and more delicate the flavor will be.

Honey comes in many forms; liquid (or pourable) honey is the most popular and prevalent. Spun honey (also called whipped or crème honey), with its delightfully creamy, spreadable texture, is also popular. Comb honey—liquid honey packed with a piece of edible wax comb, a more novel than practical version—is also available.

Because of its high sugar content, honey has a very long shelf life and will not spoil. Store it, tightly covered, in a cool, dark cupboard. If honey gets too cold, it can crystallize, becoming thick and grainy. If this happens, place the jar in a pan of hot water until it warms and liquefies again.

To measure something as sticky as honey, lightly oil your measuring cup, or spray it with a nonstick vegetable cooking spray before filling with honey. The honey will not stick to the cup and will pour right out.

Honey is sweeter than sugar, so often you can use less honey than sugar to sweeten a recipe. If you want to experiment with honey, start by substituting half of the sugar required in a recipe with honey. This will give you an idea of how you like the flavor and texture of the dish with honey added. Here are some basic guidelines for further baking with honey:

- Honey is hygroscopic, which means it draws moisture from the environment. Baked goods made with honey are usually very moist and keep well. In fact, breads or cakes made with honey are often better tasting and moister if given a little time to mellow and "age" for a day or so before eating them.

- Since honey is sweeter than sugar, substitute $3/4$ cup honey for every cup of sugar in a recipe. It also contains more

## HONEY

liquid than sugar, so for every cup of honey used, reduce the liquid in the recipe by $1/4$ cup.

- Honey is acidic, so if you are replacing sugar with honey and your recipe doesn't call for any other acidic ingredients like sour cream, buttermilk, molasses, brown sugar, or natural cocoa powder, you may want to substitute a portion of the baking powder (if it is in the recipe) with baking soda to balance the acidity in the honey.

- Recipes with honey tend to brown faster and darker than recipes using sugar. To prevent overbrowning, reduce the oven temperature by 25°F.

When I was growing up, my dad and I went often to Aiello's Delicatessen, a tiny neighborhood shop jam-packed with wonderful, and to me, exotic flavors: imported Italian meats; delicious green olives, cracked and oily and marinated in masses of garlic; shelves stacked with dusty packages of bread sticks, jars of roasted peppers, and tiny boxes of Italian *torrone*. My favorite treat was the freshly made baklava, chunky squares at least 2 inches thick, glistening with honey and resting on sticky cupcake papers. The first time you taste baklava is a revelation; it isn't candy or cake or cookie, but is simultaneously crisp, chewy, and sweet—a wonderfully serendipitous amalgamation of nuts, spices, and pastry bound into buttery, syrupy, sweet perfection. This version is reminiscent of those thick squares. Don't balk at the amount of phyllo; the added layers yield a voluptuous and elegant sweet. Forget trying to eat this with a fork—it compresses the layers. Baklava is the ultimate, albeit sticky, sensuous finger food.

# Deep-Dish Baklava MAKES 20 PIECES

**FOR THE PASTRY:**

3 CUPS FINELY CHOPPED WALNUTS

2 CUPS FINELY CHOPPED ALMONDS

2/3 CUP SUGAR

2 TEASPOONS GROUND CINNAMON

1/2 TEASPOON GROUND CARDAMOM

1/4 TEASPOON GROUND CLOVES

ABOUT 2 POUNDS PHYLLO DOUGH (SEVENTY-FIVE 9-BY-13-INCH SHEETS) (SEE PAGE 98)

1 1/2 CUPS (3 STICKS) UNSALTED BUTTER, MELTED

**FOR THE SYRUP:**

2 CUPS SUGAR

2 CUPS MILD HONEY

2 CUPS WATER

ONE 6-INCH STRIP LEMON PEEL

1 VANILLA BEAN, HALVED LENGTHWISE

1 CINNAMON STICK

PREHEAT THE OVEN TO 350°F. Lightly butter the bottom and sides of a 9-by-13-inch metal baking pan with melted butter.

TO MAKE THE PASTRY: In a small bowl, stir together the walnuts, almonds, sugar, cinnamon, cardamom, and cloves. Set aside.

ON A CLEAN WORK SURFACE, lay flat 1 sheet of phyllo and brush it lightly with melted butter. Layer 7 more sheets of phyllo over the first, buttering each one. Carefully lay this stack of buttered phyllo sheets in the prepared pan. Sprinkle evenly with 1 cup of the nut mixture. Layer together 8 more sheets of phyllo, buttering each sheet, and lay this stack over the first layer of nuts. Sprinkle the second stack of phyllo sheets with another 1 cup of the nut mixture.

REPEAT THIS PROCESS UNTIL THERE ARE 5 STACKS OF BUTTERED PHYLLO (8 SHEETS IN EACH STACK) SEPARATED BY AND ENDING WITH A LAYER OF NUT MIXTURE (1 CUP FOR EACH OF 5 LAYERS). On a flat work surface, prepare the top of the pastry by layering together 35 sheets of phyllo dough, buttering each sheet. Carefully place this stack of layered phyllo over the last layer of nuts in the pan. The pan should be completely full of pastry.

"*Honeybees are very tricky. Honey doesn't make them sticky.*"
—FROM *EGG THOUGHTS AND OTHER FRANCES SONGS*, BY RUSSELL HOBAN

WITH A SHARP KNIFE, score the baklava into square or diamond-shaped pieces by cutting through just the top layers of phyllo dough.

BAKE UNTIL CRISP THROUGHOUT AND THE TOP LAYERS ARE GOLDEN BROWN, 1 to 1½ hours.

WHILE THE BAKLAVA IS BAKING, MAKE THE HONEY SYRUP: Combine all the syrup ingredients in a large stockpot and bring the syrup to a boil over medium-high heat. Reduce the heat to medium and simmer until the mixture is the consistency of thick maple syrup, about 10 minutes. Remove the syrup from the heat and let cool slightly.

AS SOON AS THE BAKLAVA COMES OUT OF THE OVEN, spoon the slightly warm syrup over the pastry. Let the baklava cool completely before cutting the scored pieces completely. Don't be nervous if the baklava seems to be swimming in the syrup initially. As the pastry cools, the syrup is absorbed into the layers. It is very important to allow the baklava to cool completely—this gives the syrup plenty of time to ease into the pastry layers and give the baklava its wonderful gooey-crisp texture. Baklava will keep, covered, for 2 days at room temperature or 4 days refrigerated.

This traditional recipe for coppery bronzed, sweetly crunchy, caramel corn is enlivened with chewy pieces of dried, candied pineapple, shards of coconut, and buttery macadamia nuts for a fun, tropical flair. Feel free to substitute or omit any ingredients if you don't have all the ones listed below. Just take care not to add more than 3 or 4 cups of ingredients to the popcorn—if you do, you may not have enough brown-sugar caramel syrup to coat them with.

# Hawaiian Caramel Corn MAKES 16 CUPS

1/2 CUP DRIED BANANA CHIPS

1 CUP WHOLE ROASTED MACADAMIA NUTS

1 CUP UNSWEETENED FLAKED COCONUT (SEE PAGE 78)

1/2 CUP DICED CANDIED PINEAPPLE

16 TO 18 CUPS POPPED POPCORN

**FOR THE CARAMEL SYRUP:**

1 CUP (2 STICKS) UNSALTED BUTTER

1 CUP GRANULATED SUGAR

1 1/2 CUPS FIRMLY PACKED DARK BROWN SUGAR

1/2 CUP LIGHT OR DARK CORN SYRUP

1 TEASPOON FRESH LEMON JUICE

1 TEASPOON SALT

1 TEASPOON PURE VANILLA EXTRACT

1/2 TEASPOON PURE COCONUT EXTRACT (OPTIONAL)

1/2 TEASPOON BAKING SODA

PREHEAT THE OVEN TO 250°F. Spray 2 baking sheets with nonstick cooking spray and set aside.

COMBINE THE BANANA CHIPS, macadamia nuts, coconut flakes, and candied pineapple in a very large bowl. Toss to mix. Pour the popcorn into the bowl with the dried fruit. Toss with your hands to combine the mixture.

TO MAKE THE SYRUP: In a large saucepan over medium heat, combine the butter, sugars, corn syrup, lemon juice, and salt. Cook, stirring occasionally, until the butter and sugars melt together. Increase the heat to high and bring the mixture to a boil. Boil gently until the mixture reaches the hard-crack stage (300°F on a candy thermometer; see page 154), 6 to 9 minutes. Remove from the heat and stir in vanilla, coconut extract (if using), and the baking soda. The syrup will bubble and foam when the baking soda is added; simply stir until it subsides. Immediately pour the caramel over the popcorn mixture and stir with a large wooden spoon until a caramel glaze completely coats all the popped corn, nuts, and fruit.

DIVIDE THE CARAMEL CORN BETWEEN THE PREPARED BAKING SHEETS AND BAKE UNTIL THE POPCORN IS CRISP AND FRAGRANT, stirring occasionally, about 1 hour. Let cool completely before eating. The cooled caramel corn can be stored, tightly covered, for about 1 week.

## SOURCES

**THE BAKER'S CATALOGUE / KING ARTHUR FLOUR**

P.O. Box 876
Norwich, Vermont 05055-0876
800-827-6836
www.bakerscatalogue.com

Baking equipment and pans, chocolates, cocoa powders, confectionery coating, premium vanilla extracts and other extracts, specialty flours and sugars

**DURKEE-MOWER, INC.**

P.O. Box 470
Lynn, Massachusetts 01903
781-593-8007
www.marshmallowfluff.com

Marshmallow Fluff and other Fluff products

**INDIA TREE**

1421 Elliott Avenue West
Seattle, Washington 98119
800-369-4848
www.indiatree.com

Raw muscovado, demerara, and turbinado sugars; decorative sanding sugars

**NEW YORK CAKE SUPPLIES**

56 West 22nd Street
New York, New York 10010
212-675-CAKE
www.nycake.com

Cake, muffin, and assorted tart and pie pans; cake decorating supplies; pastry bags and tips

**PENZEYS SPICES**

19300 West Janacek Court
P.O. Box 924
Brookfield, Wisconsin 53008-0924
262-785-7676
www.penzeys.com

Spices, extracts, whole vanilla beans and double-strength vanilla extract

**SWEET CELEBRATIONS**

P.O. Box 39426
Edina, Minnesota 55439-0426
800-328-6722
www.sweetc.com

Bakeware, cake decorating and candy-making supplies, lollipop sticks, caramel, chocolates and confectionery coating, desiccated (macaroon) coconut

**WILLIAMS-SONOMA, INC.**

Mail Order Department
P.O. Box 7456
San Francisco, California 94102-7456
800-541-2233
www.williams-sonoma.com

Top-quality assorted cake pans, tart pans, cake and cookie decorating supplies, measuring cups, spoons, mixers, bowls, knives, European chocolates and cocoa powders, quality extracts, vanilla beans and sugars

# Table of Equivalents

The exact equivalents in the following tables have been rounded for convenience.

## LIQUID/DRY MEASUREMENTS

| U.S. | METRIC |
| --- | --- |
| 1/4 teaspoon | 1.25 milliliters |
| 1/2 teaspoon | 2.5 milliliters |
| 1 teaspoon | 5 milliliters |
| 1 tablespoon (3 teaspoons) | 15 milliliters |
| 1 fluid ounce (2 tablespoons) | 30 milliliters |
| 1/4 cup | 60 milliliters |
| 1/3 cup | 80 milliliters |
| 1/2 cup | 120 milliliters |
| 1 cup | 240 milliliters |
| 1 pint (2 cups) | 480 milliliters |
| 1 quart (4 cups, 32 ounces) | 960 milliliters |
| 1 gallon (4 quarts) | 3.84 liters |
| 1 ounce (by weight) | 28 grams |
| 1 pound | 448 grams |
| 2.2 pounds | 1 kilogram |

## LENGTHS

| U.S. | METRIC |
| --- | --- |
| 1/8 inch | 3 millimeters |
| 1/4 inch | 6 millimeters |
| 1/2 inch | 12 millimeters |
| 1 inch | 2.5 centimeters |

## OVEN TEMPERATURE

| FAHRENHEIT | CELSIUS | GAS |
| --- | --- | --- |
| 250 | 120 | 1/2 |
| 275 | 140 | 1 |
| 300 | 150 | 2 |
| 325 | 160 | 3 |
| 350 | 180 | 4 |
| 375 | 190 | 5 |
| 400 | 200 | 6 |
| 425 | 220 | 7 |
| 450 | 230 | 8 |
| 475 | 240 | 9 |
| 500 | 260 | 10 |